Greyhound Tales

True Stories of Rescue, Compassion & Love

Edited by Nora Star

Inception by Kari Mastrocola

Lost Coast Press

〰

Fort Bragg, California

Greyhound Tales: True Stories of Rescue, Compassion & Love

Copyright © 1997 by Nora Star

Lost Coast Press
155 Cypress Street
Fort Bragg, California 95437

(707) 964-9520
http://www.cypresshouse.com

ISBN 1-882897-18-8

Design & production by Cypress House
Fort Bragg, California

Cover design by Colored Horse Studios
Elk, California

Cover photos
Front: Kim Owens
Back (top) and spine: Susan Netboy
Back (bottom): Lauren Emery

Printed by Hignell Printing
Winnipeg, Manitoba, Canada

First edition

Dedication

This book is dedicated to every greyhound on the planet... we hope that this book will improve the quality of your lives. And to those already in greyhound heaven, we apologize for not getting there in time.

Table of Contents

Foreword

The soul is the same in all living creatures. . .
only the body is different."

— *Hippocrates*

As you read a few of our stories and some of the history, you will learn a little more about these wondrous dogs and the circumstances that surround them. Although adoption, of course, is not a final solution, we believe it is a helpful stop-gap measure to be used until such time as public morality dictates that we stop exploiting these dogs by racing. Until that time, anyone who has the good fortune to adopt one or more will be forever changed by the experience.

There is a resource list at the end of this book for any of you who want to become more involved, whether by adopting or helping the cause in some other way.

Nora has been involved with many animal welfare concerns, but her association with these dogs, their owners, and the many rescue workers, has impressed her more than any other. She is thankful to each and every person doing whatever they can to help these magnificent beings to regain some of the dignity and respect they so richly deserve. Her experiences while fostering various greyhounds were heartrending and profound. The way the dogs maintained their trust and faith in people after living such isolated and mechanized lives truly amazed her.

This collection is from those who were willing to share their stories. We wanted all who have a story to find a voice in this book, but we were disappointed to find that many of the excellent writers felt it necessary to withdraw their stories. Why? Because their "connections" at various racetracks throughout the country would be lost. These people pick up dogs for adoption. Their associates who facilitate this would no longer continue to do so if their anti-racing feelings were made public in this book. The phenomenon was far more prevalent than we had imagined. Even when we offered to publish their stories anonymously they declined. The threat still remained.

We thank all of you for your cooperation and creativity, for the wonderful poetry, stories, photographs, drawings, and for your patience as this work has finally come to completion.

— Nora Star and Kari Mastrocola,
who will always be friends to greyhounds

Introduction

Susan Netboy

THE GREYHOUND RACING DOG has been the beneficiary of the most successful single-breed rescue mission in the history of the animal welfare movement. This unparalleled effort has not only reinstated the greyhound to its rightful place as a highly esteemed companion animal, but it has also forced an entire industry to acknowledge the need to incorporate humane principles into its business practices.

Although racing greyhounds continue to die in numbers that will never be acceptable, in recent years rescuers have been able to save many more as thousands of adopters open their hearts and homes to these beautiful, gentle dogs. Most adopters, however, know little of the often harrowing efforts behind the rescue of their new pet; and they are even less aware of the hard work and personal sacrifices made by the individuals involved in the greyhound rescue movement.

Greyhound Tales gives the reader a sense of the remarkable resilience and good nature of the greyhound, as well as insight into the hearts and minds of the extraordinary individuals who devote their lives to saving greyhound racing dogs. Greyhound rescue is a life of long days, endless chores, and often agonizing choices about who will live and who will die. For now, the joy of watching survivors arrive at a safe haven must suffice to ward off the haunting images of those left behind. Ultimately the fate of future generations of racing dogs lies with those who are willing and able to share their experiences, for it is their courage that will provide the most compelling deterrent to a tragic repetition of history. While *Greyhound Tales* tells some of these success stories, countless others, no less heroic in their scope and impact, go on day after day. These valiant efforts are carried out not only by those who may happen to step into the media limelight but also by hundreds of other dedicated souls who work quietly behind the scenes providing the support, determination and finances to make it all possible.

Energized by images of the little muzzled faces who wait in the wings, volunteers work tirelessly to find more and more of those special homes where the innate trust and devotion of the greyhound will be rewarded with a lifetime of love.

Masay and the Rescue from Mallorca

B. Anne Finch

The time will come when public opinion will no longer tolerate
amusements based on the mistreatment and killing of animals.
— *Albert Schweitzer*

IN JULY 1991 a horrific, heartrending article appeared in a
national newspaper about Irish greyhounds exported to
Spain for racing. I knew of the scandal and had been en-
gaged in campaigning against the export for some time.
The large center page picture of Masay, a red-eyed, panting,
exhausted black greyhound slumped in a cage unable to
stand up even before she was due to race, tore me to pieces.
I felt someone had to go to Spain, face the Spanish and —
dare I even hope — find the poor bitch and bring her to
England. I had all sorts of ideas as to who should go. Was it to
be the vet, a priest, a greyhound trainer? I found no one who
would go. In the meantime, I made tentative inquiries with
British Airways and quarantine kennels about costs and at first

1

it seemed all too depressing and expensive and bound up in red tape. Suddenly the miracles started to happen. British Airways offered free passage from Barcelona for three dogs worth $700; Raystede Animal Welfare Centre offered three free quarantine places worth $3000; and Willowslea Quarantine Kennels offered travel boxes valued at $300. While hardly realizing it, I personally was becoming deeply involved and reluctantly had to admit that it had to be me or no one who would be going. I was scared out of my wits. I'd never been to Spain and spoke no Spanish.

I'd already decided that Mallorca was the only place where one stood a chance of rescuing three dogs. Even there, problems abounded. Mallorca is an island and British Airways only flew as far as Barcelona. The regulation size of the boxes was too high to fit into the cargo holds of nearly all of Iberia's internal flights to Mallorca. Also, where would I store the boxes secretly in Mallorca? Even one box would not fit into a taxi. How would I transport and house the dogs once I'd got them? I planned, worried, sweat and wrung my hands every night for the 6 weeks coming up to the date of departure. I only slept one night in four.

Another miracle happened shortly before leaving. A Spanish lady, Marisa, whom I knew slightly at my place or work, and who had lived in England for twenty years, said she would come with me. Her strength of character, sense of humor and positive attitude were all to be invaluable.

I was encouraged the night before leaving when Marisa unexpectedly got a telephone call from an old friend she had not heard from in 9 years! And where was she these days? In Barcelona, for goodness sake, asking when Marisa would come over and see her! "I've got news for you," Marisa said, "I'll be in Barcelona tomorrow night and we are in desperate need of help!" We had the three huge boxes and nowhere to spend the night while waiting for the connecting flight to Mallorca. Fortunately, Marisa's friend met us, sorted it all out and took us back to her flat. This bit of good luck made me feel that fate had a hand in this project and that 'someone' was looking after us.

Early the next morning we went on to Palma, Mallorca, not without a lot of persuasive talking from Marisa, as Iberia Airlines had decided to change their minds about allowing these huge boxes on the plane. On arriving in Palma, we begged to be allowed to leave the boxes in the cargo section of the airport. It took literally hours of talking and persistence as we were passed from one official to another. They all refused to help us, saying that this simply was not done, until by chance I spied a box belonging to someone else sitting in the cargo. In the end they had to agree that the boxes could be left there after all.

This left us free to go into Palma to find the kennels. We first found the greyhound stadium and then, like Sherlock Holmes, followed the dog droppings on the pavement to the area where they were housed. We came across a dilapidated collection of shanty dwellings. We learned later that there were 250 dogs kept there. We rehearsed what I was going to say. My story was that I lived in Northern Spain and wanted to buy three greyhounds as pets. I figured that to offer money for the dogs was the quickest and simplest way of rescuing them. An old man called Pedro emerged from his shack with a little fawn bitch called Matilde. She would cost $35. I accepted her, made a fuss over her and then Pedro invited me inside to choose two more at $70 each. There were fifteen to twenty dogs in that shed, some in cages, some just tied to the wall. Most were silent and lifeless, lying on hard surfaces. In one corner was a blue bitch who trembled from head to foot in a constant state of terror. I chose her and another bitch called Linda. It was important to get any away as fast as possible. Amazingly, Pedro handed me the racing documents which testified in every shocking detail how often the dogs had been running per week and how they ran through their seasons. At one worrying moment, Marisa had to do some fast talking. Pedro saw the smart greyhound collars we were putting on the dogs and asked where we got them. It hadn't occurred to me that they were not available in Spain!

I'd heard of kennels twenty miles away run by Linda, an English lady. We hired a car, then, out of sight of the hire company, loaded the dogs. We set out to find the kennels. The dogs were alive with fleas. On arrival, we hosed the dogs down. The fleas were crawling up my arms. The dogs had large bald patches on their rears, due to stress and the hard surfaces on which they had lain. The vet, a very kind Argentinean, came to do the necessary vaccinations, worming and health certifications for export.

It remained for us to go to the vet at the Ministry of Agriculture in Palma to obtain the final certificates for export. Nothing was easy. It was a complicated drive and finding the right office was a nightmare. One could tell that nothing like this had been done before. Finally, our work was completed. We had only 2 more days before leaving.

Meanwhile, we visited the greyhound track and observed what went on there. Many dogs had skin diseases — I had never seen *pink* greyhounds before — and many were lame before the race even started. We saw one dog have its number changed and raced for a second time that evening. In Britain dogs only race once every 7-10 days. None of the usual paddock procedures took place such as washing the sand from the dogs' feet and eyes after racing or even giving them water to drink. We talked to several people to get as much information as possible.

Suddenly I saw Masay, the black bitch featured in the newspaper article who had inspired me to go to Spain in the first place. There she was, slumped in her pre-racing box exactly as she had been a few weeks earlier when the press were there. The bandages on her wrists were the same. I compared her with the photo. It was she, all right. I became riveted and desperate, while Marisa tried to talk sense into me and told me to forget about it. We only had documents, quarantine places and passage for three and an airplane could only take three. But I couldn't take my eyes off her. Marisa tried to shake me out of my obsession and suggested that we go to a flamenco show that night. I'd never heard flamenco music before and really didn't feel in the mood. Furthermore, it didn't begin until 1:00 a.m. which I found excruciating as I am always up at 6:00 a.m. Nevertheless, we went.

Then something startling happened. The Gypsy singer stood up and uttered her first guttural, earthy sound, more like a wail from the heart than a song, and I disgraced myself by suddenly dissolving into paroxysms of uncontrollable sobbing. Never did I expect that the music would echo what I was feeling inside, that it would trigger such a disastrous response. I was quite out of control and after half-an-hour of trying to get hold of myself I finally had to leave.

Back at the hotel, it occurred to me, piece by piece, what I could do. Yes, I would try to get her out of the hovel and take her to Linda's kennels. It occurred to me that Matilde's condition was not that bad and she could wait and be sent over later when I'd sorted out more paperwork.

We were running out of time. Marisa this time took fright and wouldn't come anywhere near the kennels. She was sure I'd be shot, going in for a second time! I went in, and stuttered away in a sort of Hispanic mixture of French and Italian. Pedro said Masay was owned by the manager of the track. I realized

I would have problems procuring her. I met the manager later that evening and asked him how much she would cost. I expected him to say something like $30, as she was obviously so weak and poor, but he said 35,000 pesetas (about $200) which was extortionate, ridiculous, and obviously designed to put me off. (The Spanish only pay $50 each for the dogs in Ireland when they are fresh and young.) I gulped at this, but so badly wanted her that I'd resolved not to argue about the price. How could I afford this? The cost of the trip was ruining me. That morning I had drawn more money out on credit and I'd grabbed a wad of bills on leaving the hotel that evening and put them in a secret pocket. I was still unfamiliar with the currency so I hadn't a clue what I had. I counted up what was there and to my amazement found I had *exactly* 35,000 pesetas. I immediately felt certain that I was *meant* to have that dog. I called his bluff and astonished him by immediately handing him the money. He could do nothing else to prevent me from having her. We hired another car and rushed her away, and then had to go through the hoop again of finding Linda's kennels in the hills, calling the vet and going to the Ministry of Agriculture. Because of the shortage of time, we had to do things backwards. Masay had not yet been seen by the vet and vaccinated. The Ministry closed at lunchtime for the day so we went there first and submitted the paperwork but in desperation I handed the Ministry vet another dog's paperwork and hoped and prayed that he wouldn't see that the color of the dog didn't tally. I distracted him by keeping him talking. It worked. He signed it. We'd done it.

Afterwards, we took Masay to the vet and the formalities were properly carried out. One slight hiccup was that I thought she ought to be tested for Leishmaniasis as she was in poor condition. If she had it, she would be euthanised in quarantine and the trip would have been wasted. Thankfully, the test came back negative. We had finished.

The next morning we had to get up at 4:00 a.m. to get the dogs to the air terminal. But a minor disaster struck. I had lost my memory! Yes — I awoke quite disorientated and didn't even know which country I was in or what I was doing with these dogs! The stress of the last six weeks had finally caught up with me. Marisa took over while I tried to appear sane and we got the dogs into their boxes and checked them in for the internal flight to Barcelona. I drank pints of coffee and finally after five hours, thankfully my wits returned, as we landed in Barcelona.

From then on, British Airways, bless them, took over and apart from being struck twice by lightning on the flight back, we landed safely at Heathrow, with the quarantine van waiting on the tarmac.

The dogs all did well in quarantine and were finally homed to loving and caring owners. Matilde arrived a month later.

The bad publicity I gave to what I had seen caused the World Greyhound Federation to suspend the trade between Ireland and Spain for five months pending an inspection of the three greyhound establishments in Spain, and Mallorca's kennels were ordered to close. New kennels were built at a very inconvenient site inland. The dogs are still kept in cages without bedding, air-conditioning, piped water or a proper electricity source. Much work still needs to be done. I went to Spain 10 more times to all three tracks and kennels taking in many suitcases of veterinary equipment, liniments, bandages, instructive videos, etc. and worked in the kennels de-infecting the dogs and dressing their wounds. I've managed to get 25 dogs to England, Germany and Switzerland to loving caring homes.

Dear Masay went to a lovely home in Norfolk. After two

years there she tragically did develop Leishmaniasis after all as it was latent. She bore her illness so bravely but was finally euthanized in November 1994.

She was one of those very special dogs who seemed wise and aware of what she represented and instigated.

The Only Choice

Kim Owens

> Some of our greatest historical and artistic treasures we
> place in museums. . .others we take for walks.
> — *Roger A. Caras*

MY HUSBAND ROBERT and I are just crazy about our three
adopted greyhounds but their adoption came about in an un-
usual way. Now we would not take any amount of money for
our dogs, but in the beginning we had no idea that we would
be changed forever. As our story unfolds, you will see that we
really had only one choice to make!

It all started about two years ago with a conversation on
greyhounds. We had a friend who worked at a kennel in Florida,
and she would return home to our area occasionally to visit. I
have been an animal lover all of my life, but I must admit that
the plight of retired racers had somehow passed me by. Robert and I weren't aware of what was happening, or about the
various rescue efforts happening all over the country. As our
friend told us all this, I found myself petting the large grey-

hound with her who was already leaning heavily on my legs. Neither one of us could take our eyes off "King" who was destined for an arranged adoption. Those big golden eyes had me and I could barely tear myself away. Two minutes petting a sick dog and my life was changed forever. We hadn't thought about getting another dog for our menagerie at home, so this presented a whole new ballgame. She told us to think about it, because the choice is truly a long term one. She would be coming home again soon, and could bring us a dog. We exchanged phone numbers and I promised to call. Before she left, she gave me the wonderful book *Adopting the Racing Greyhound* by Branigan. "Read this," she said, "then call me. We'll talk about it."

As our conversations continued over the next few weeks, Robert and I both worried. What about our busy lifestyle, my love of indoor cats, or the expense of adopting dogs with potential health problems? Although most adoptions are done through agencies, we were starting from scratch, heading for experiences unknown to us. My usual response to uncertainty, however, is to do research. I began calling vets and learned the cost of various procedures. I read books, looked up articles, and generally became obsessed with the idea of owning one of these wonderful creatures. After several weeks, we realized the idea wouldn't go away and made the call to our friend. She told us the owner she worked with had three dogs available. Although they were personal favorites, none of them could make it as runners. One dog had been kept far longer than usual because the owner liked her and hated to put her down. At eighteen months the three littermates were already washed up and out of the business. Our friend promised a delivery when she had homes arranged for the other two.

We set about getting ready for the first needy "baby" in our home. I chose my vet carefully after finding one nearby who had actually worked in the racing kennels in California. His partner had worked there too. What a stroke of luck to have two greyhound familiar vets in one office. I read Branigan's book again, and we fenced in the back yard of our country home. I bought treats and talked with my vet about dog food and what sorts of problems to expect. To this day I am an info-fanatic with all sorts of "greyhound goodies" file folders.

Finally the big day arrived! Our friend called us to meet her at the front of our property. Robert rushed out, without so much as a backward glance at me as I finished dressing. When I reached her van I was utterly amazed. They were the prettiest things I had ever seen! Every time they would turn their heads they would try to kiss each other through their muzzles. A car sped by and the big male spun around to place himself between the danger and the two females behind him. They had obviously bonded to each other during the trip after being isolated for so much of their lives, but we sorted them out finally to hear their stories. Stubby, a fawn female, was so named because her tail had been caught in a door when she was just a pup, leaving it a few inches shorter. She had never made it past her training races, but had been kept by the owner for six more months. Angel, the big red brindle male, immediately seemed to want my complete attention and was very reluctant to move away. Sunshine, a tiny red fawn female, seemed to wiggle all the time and had to get her nose on everything around her. Although she had been fast on the track, she had been far more interested in playing with all the other dogs and had caused a few accidents.

Now, all we had to do was pick the one we wanted. It seemed like an easy task. But Robert was looking at me with big moon eyes and pitiful appeals. He liked the friendly little wiggle-butt, Sunshine, the best. Yet, here I had this big strapping tiger-striped dog doing his best to wrap himself around my legs. The worst part of all was the way they cried and struggled when we separated them from each other. Our friend looked at me once and said gently "Do you really *want* to separate them?" The idea hadn't even occurred to us but the possibility came in a blinding flash. You guessed it already — all of a sudden we were the proud owners of three rescued racing greyhounds! There was no way in the world any of those dogs were getting back in that van.

We are very lucky, because our story has the very best of endings. It could have turned out much differently. I had done my research well and knew ahead of time what would be required. We have four acres of land, and no children to need attention. We own an antique store and I teach school so we can afford the additional expenses. We didn't have the advantage of the services offered by an adoption group, but we were working directly with the trainer who knew the dogs well enough to pick some for us. In the end, the money and concern never came close to the joy and wonder they brought to our home. Multiple adoptions have the advantage that the dogs keep each other company and learn from the rewards given to the others. Although we started with mostly "outside" dogs (South Carolina is very mild), they were so easy to get along with that they soon became part of the house whenever we were home. We didn't even have chewing and housetraining problems after the rules were reinforced a bit. The cat soon learned that they were bigger than she was and the dogs in turn learned that although that furry thing was really aggravating, mommy and daddy wouldn't let you eat it. Of course we had to take things slowly and learned along with the dogs mostly by trial and error. Every second was worth it. Never in my life have I known dogs who work their way so quickly into your heart. They must love being with us too. One night my husband woke in the middle of the night and was horrified to find the back door on the "dog porch" (their sleeping spot) had blown wide open. Judging by the leaves inside, it had been that way for some time. All three dogs were curled up together asleep, however, less than two feet from freedom. Our hearts skipped several beats, but we took our luck that night as a good sign from above.

Have you guessed yet which dog became our favorite? She is always quiet, loves nothing better than to sleep in the living room touching us. When she has the chance she runs the fastest. She always comes to us for attention first, even when there is food waiting. She is patient and will stand for the longest time (without being irritating) hoping to get a rub. Give her a rawhide bone and she won't touch another thing in the house. Take her in our shop and she walks straight to her rug before going to sleep, only moving if someone wants to pet her. If I could only have one, she would be it. The dog is Stubby, of course; the one we didn't want at first. She'll never feel lonely and forgotten again.

Demi: Death in the Rain Diverted

Louise Coleman

> You think dogs will not be in heaven?
> I tell you, they will be there long before any of us.
> — *Robert Louis Stevenson*

IT WAS A dark green, pungent place with the long-ago dead in rows. Someone walked there in the rain and cold and saw the misery of a little dog who was wired to a gravestone. So a call came to the Irish Society for the Prevention of Cruelty to Animals about a small greyhound tied to a stone and suffering. The whispery voice gave the barest of facts, and could not give a name because, it said, "they will come to kill my animals." It was a raw gray November 10, the death time of the year. Some dogs end up abused by cruelty, made to quiver, to start to cower, to dodge, to flee. The most tender, the most vulnerable suffer.

When Marion Fitzgibbon, Chairwoman of the ISPCA, came to search, the GARDA (Irish police) told her "There is no greyhound in St. Lawrence's. No such being exists. You're misinformed, Missus, you're wasting your time." But Marion believed the voice that had called. She knew a little dog was in there. The voice had given the section, row and stone. Marion and her companion, Beverly, went in the dark November afternoon to search. The area was empty, of life, filled with piles of red and brown leaves. Just as they were leaving, out of the leaves came the head of a small red and white greyhound. Help had come at the last moment; she would not have lived another day. Her small spirit was strong but it was being bled away. The days were dark; there was no renewal or comfort from the sun. She had heard the women walking but remained hidden because she was afraid of human footsteps. Then she became brave and she could probably see the two good women looking for her. Her dark, cold nights were over. The little dog had been deliberately put in the graveyard, wired to a tombstone, and left to die. There is a *demi* — half and half, the beauty and the horror of the world. When the usual controls are gone,

> Things fall apart: the center cannot hold;
> Mere anarchy is loosed upon the world,
> The blood dimmed tide is loosed, and
> everywhere the ceremony of innocence is drowned.
> — *W.B. Yeats, 1921*

From now on the little dog would be blessed with the best care. She was taken to Glenlohane, the home of Desmond and Melanie Sharp Bolster. She was named "Demi" by Melanie because she was half red and half white. The name also seemed appropriate because when she was found she was half alive, half dead. At Glenlohane, she lived in a bathroom where she felt most safe, and the companion who kept her company was a Corgi. Desmond carried her upstairs in a blanket in the evening to the bedroom so she could be watched over.

Melanie and Desmond healed Demi's physical wounds: an elegant young greyhound emerged from a freezing, starved, filthy dog. But she could make no eye contact with any person, would not take the most tasty morsel from a human hand, and she cringed at even the gentlest touch.

Then Jill Hopfenbeck and I went to Ireland to attend a meeting of Irish people interested in beginning an adoption program for Irish greyhounds. Jill had first seen a greyhound in her Tufts Veterinary School anatomy class — several greyhounds laid out for dissection.

We met Demi and decided she would have her best chance at a normal life by emigrating to the United States. With the prejudice that exists in Ireland against greyhounds as pets, a suitable home would be almost impossible to find for her there. In a farewell letter that accompanied Demi on her flight from Ireland:

I feel confident that Demi will meet someone very special who will love her and care for her in the way that she so desperately needs. Greyhound Friends has so many more people to draw from and Demi's chances of running free and finding some happiness is far greater with you than with me in Ireland. Demi came to us a broken-spirited and sick creature. She will be going out to you physically well but still emotionally scarred. I am glad she will be with you, Jill, as I know your calm and caring way will help her. It is late now, after midnight, and Demi and I are going to make an early start in the morning. She will hardly understand what her trip is all about but maybe someday she will be able to look you in the eye and smile her thanks to you.

Like so many Irish immigrants who came before her, Demi's resurrection began with a cold, dark terrifying journey into the unknown. Her leave-taking was an emotional one for both Marion and Melanie. They found her and put her back together physically, and now they were sending her off to her destiny in the New World, where they hoped that she could heal her considerable emotional wounds. Melanie wished that Demi would be "fleet of foot" in her recovery. They waited with her in the cargo area at Shannon Airport on that raw January morning, and tried to reassure her as they placed a muzzle on her face. They loaded her into her travel crate, a mere 18" wide, but those are the rules for greyhounds on Aer Lingus. ("Of course, if she were a *domestic dog*, now, she wouldn't have to travel muzzled," we were told by Aer Lingus officials). When we picked her up at the cargo terminal in Boston, she hadn't moved for the entire 7-hour trip. She was frozen in fear, wondering what new tortures man had dreamed up for her to endure.

Jill adopted Demi. Demi loved Jill's other greyhounds and the mutt, Jake, a happy playmate. Over a year and a half, Demi slowly came out of her shell, and began to trust people. When she first arrived at Jill's house, she would not move from her bed, unless it was to rush slinking outside. If someone came into the room, she would slam her body against the wall and roll up into her most defensive position, averting her eyes. There were glimmers of hope: she played happily with Jill's other dogs, and learned the joy of a New England winter and running in the snow. As spring came, she began to show small signs of growing trust: submissively licking a hand, taking a special treat, and finally tentatively approaching Jill of her own free will to be patted. Never, despite all her fears, did she ever show the slightest sign of aggression. The gentle trusting side of her nature made her experience in the graveyard all the more horrible in retrospect — what kind of monster could walk her into the cemetery, wire her collar to a gravestone and leave her to die?

Every day, Demi makes strides on her road to becoming a "real dog." Once she had some confidence, she began obedience training, and this structure has given her a means to control her fears. That worked so well that Demi, now registered with the AKC as "Glenlohane Demi," is about to begin competitive obedience trails. She now knows how to play with both people and dogs, and goes to work with Jill every day in order to meet as many strangers as possible. While the world still worries Demi, you can see, day by day, the nightmare fading, and being replaced by the love and confidence that is every dog's birthright.

Demi should have the dog Medal of Honor.

Susie's Story

Bobbi Wolner

Life is as dear to a mute creature as it is to a man.
Just as one wants happiness and fears pain, just as
one wants to live and not die, so do other creatures.
— *His Holiness the Dalai Lama*

She was absolutely breathtaking, this fawn colored two-year-old greyhound with soft brown eyes that reminded me of that gentlest of creatures, the deer. In those soulful eyes one saw pain, fear, absolute terror. She could not say it in words but her eyes and body expressed it. She trembled at a person's touch, her body going rigid; ready for flight and hiding. Men's voices especially made her try to hide anywhere, just to escape. This was the creature I was to foster long-term, to help her become a "normal" dog.

Her life began somewhere in Arizona, beginning a racing career, but she wouldn't chase rabbits. So she was put on a truck that was to take her and eleven others to their deaths. Somehow she was rescued by Greyhounds Friends For Life.

I had seen the plight of the greyhounds on the news and had been terribly upset by the grisly findings in an orchard in Arizona. The time had come to do more than just feel anger and outrage and so, when I saw the number for Greyhound Friends For Life, I called. It seemed wisest to volunteer first to foster a greyhound and that is how I met Susie. She was being fostered by Nora but needed to stay someplace for as long as it took to bring her around.

Nora and I set a date for meeting on a Sunday and I drove to her home in a state of excitement and some trepidation. After all, I already had a six-year-old Norwegian elkhound mix and ten cats at home. Would Susie be able to adapt to this menagerie?

Meeting Susie was quite an experience. She was so fearful that she shook and wanted to hide rather than have me look at her. She was in absolute agony hoping to escape into the back room again. Those eyes, however, had me hooked and I told Nora that I would be willing to foster her for the six months or year that it might take to help.

Nora filled me in on Susie's background. She and eleven other greyhounds had been rescued from a "death" truck in Arizona. She was not quite two years old at that time but would not chase rabbits and was of no further use to the kennel. It was obvious that she had been badly mistreated since she would flinch when touched and was afraid of almost everything, but especially of men's voices. Her tail looked as if it had been broken and she had cysts on her front left elbow. By the August Sunday when I first saw her, she had already been fostered for several months but needed a long term home. I decided to commit to whatever time it would take. I knew she deserved a better life than she had experienced in her first two years.

Nora sent me on my way with Susie and her muzzle (as a

safeguard for my cats). I live in the Santa Cruz mountains and the ride home was a long one but Susie did well in the car. My home, however, was a real challenge. I live on a hillside and access to my front door is up many stairs to a deck. Racing greyhounds are not familiar with stairs or mirrors or glass doors or the insides of homes. At first Susie practically had to be carried up the stairs (which is difficult since she weighs 74 pounds and is as large as a good-sized male). Forget about coming down the stairs. A circuitous route had to be improvised which included a ramp to the cellar window, a trip through the cellar and out its door in order to reach the gate and get the reward of going hiking with me and Charlie, my resident dog.

I also chose not to crate Susie or muzzle her. I wanted her to begin her new life as a normal dog. My cats knew and understood dogs and were cautious in getting close to Susie. She proved to be gentle with all of them from the very first day. Crating was not needed because she had a cave-like place to hide in the bedroom in the narrow space between my bed and the wall. Now all I had to do was convince her that life could — no — *would* be good.

Time truly does heal wounds. With a lot of help from Charlie, Susie began to change. At first, on our walks, Charlie pulled and sniffed, and greeted all the neighbor dogs while Susie kept her eyes straight ahead and never pulled or tugged on her lead. She chose to ignore other dogs and I had my doubts about her abilities as a sighthound, since she never noticed deer grazing in the meadow or rabbits or squirrels nearby. Under Charlie's tutelage, however, Susie began to realize there was something out there and that it might be fun to look and sniff. The real breakthrough came when Susie smelled something delicious on a walk and decided to roll in it. To most people that would be disgusting; to me it was wonderful because Susie was showing "real" dog traits.

Another breakthrough came when Susie required surgery on her front left elbow for a cyst that had begun to grow and which my veterinarian feared was cancerous. Fortunately, the cyst was benign but Susie was a difficult patient. She would chew off her bandages and work on the stitches. I had no choice but to confine her and the best method of confinement proved to be the back of my little Acura Integra coupe. Susie went to work with me almost every day for a month and stayed quiet while I worked. (Sometimes Charlie came too.) Breaks and lunch found me lavishing attention upon my well-bandaged dog, taking her for walks, introducing her to staff, and otherwise spending quality time. It was late October and often rainy so confinement in the car was not a problem; on sunny days I parked under the trees and opened the sunroof. During that time I took many weekend trips to Chico to visit my son, Joe, and I always brought Susie and Charlie. There are many places to hike in and around Chico and as Susie healed she could run free and play with my son's dog, a 120 pound malamute/German shepherd mix. Joe's home has an enormous backyard where the dogs had even more pleasurable times.

Susie's leg healed well and so has her spirit. She will never be a highly sociable dog but she has come a long way from the fearful and timid creature I first met. She often smiles (look closely at the picture — that is a happy dog at my son's home in Chico!) and relaxes easily around the house. Her favorite spot is the sofa — she does leave a part of a cushion for me — and she has a few favorite cats with whom she communes. She and Charlie love to travel and will accompany me on many future vacations. How lucky I was to be able to adopt Susie and watch the unfolding of the "real" dog within.

Desert Dogs

Alex Dugan

In this world, a man must be either anvil or hammer.
— *Longfellow*

I DROVE FROM California to Arizona in the spring that I finished high school. My uncle Vic had a big ranch there and I'd always wanted to spend a little time with him. As I drove into his mile-long driveway and closed the gate, I saw a herd of three-foot-tall bodies, clouded in dust, moving toward me at incredible speed. I could only hope that they were friendly, whatever they were! I didn't even have time to get back into my car, so I just stood there in awe as they loomed before me. They stopped and did the most impressive group butt-wiggling and tail-wagging I have ever seen. It was pretty clear that Uncle Vic did not have any watchdogs here! It slowly penetrated that these were greyhounds. I had only seen pictures but had never met one. What amazing spirits they had, each one a beauty in his or her own right. Then I saw Vic come sauntering down the driveway with a big toothy grin.

"You like my family?" he asked.

"Why didn't you tell me about them on the phone?" I asked back.

"Just like to keep a few surprises, and knew they'd give you a much more royal welcome than I could ever muster. They race these dogs in this state you know, and lots of them get dumped out in the desert when they no longer earn the big bucks. Lots of them are dropped with their muzzles still on so they don't even have a chance to bag a rabbit or something to stay alive."

"God that's awful, aren't there laws about that?"

"There are, but who's out on the desert to enforce 'em? Anyhow, this is how I got my family here. Every time I saw one of them in my travels, I'd pick it up and bring it home, one at a time, over three years. Lots of the ranchers around here shoot 'em, they're so scraggly lookin' but I never could do that. And, you know it *might* be my imagination, but I don't think so, they are forever grateful. They know they could never make it out there for very long. I hear tell there are packs of them living in the real remote areas where the caves are, but I've never seen 'em. Folks say they've gone wild, learned to stay out of sight of man for evermore. Bring the car up to the house and I'll make you some of my real special coffee, I even grind the beans myself!"

As I drove down the driveway toward the house, the dogs passed me easily and were in the ranch house relaxing on the cool tile by the time I walked in. A few tails thumped lazily, but it was pretty clear that it was serious nap time for this group. As we sipped our coffee and looked over the amazing collection of greyhounds here, I could see the variety. There was a large black male, about 80 pounds, and a small bony fawn male; the rest were females. One white with black spots, and the other three were brindles, which Vic told me was the most common color. I couldn't help but feel a sense of harmony among them, and including Vic and me.

"There's something special about them, all right." Vic said as if he had been reading my mind. "I've never seen anything like these dogs and I have had lots of wonderful dogs in my 50 years. These kids are so angelic, sweet, playful, affectionate, and *smart*. Boy, howdy, are they smart! It's embarrassing to be outsmarted by a dog, but it happens a lot with these guys."

Uncle Vic was as crusty as ever, but happier than I'd seen him. These dogs seemed to fill the void in his life that began when my aunt died.

"You're right about that too, sonny." He said out of the blue, reading my mind again. "There is no finer company than these dogs when you live alone. They keep you happy all the time. Every time I think of those guys dropping these dogs off like that, like so much garbage, I just want to go to the track and scream over the loudspeaker, 'STOP DOG RACES NOW!!!' Of course they'd take me to jail or the funny farm, but if it did the trick, it would be worth it! Meanwhile, I just send any extra money I can to those people who are organized and trying to do it their civilized way."

"I didn't know about any of this stuff, Vic," I said sheepishly. "We don't have dog racing in California."

"Well, you people are a lot more evolved and a lot less greedy than we Arizonans then."

As we rode the range on horseback that evening, with the dogs up ahead, I had lots to ponder. Spending that week with Vic and his dogs convinced me that my first dog would be a greyhound. I was in love with these dogs. I had always been able to take or leave dogs before — but not these dogs. As I was driving home after my visit I passed near Phoenix and for some reason was pulled to the racetrack just like a magnet. It was late and most of the people were gone, but I went in anyway. I walked down a hall with offices and saw a female fawn greyhound standing on a table, trembling while a man filled a syringe. I rushed into the office and asked if I could have the dog. He answered, "She no good to me, take her!"

Two years old and washed up. What a tragedy! I wonder how many died that day because no one walked by. I felt exhilarated to have saved this little beauty. She had come *so close* to death.

As we rode home across the desert, the greyhound lying on the seat next to me, I knew now what Uncle Vic had meant by grateful. There was no mistaking that look in her eyes. She was shy at first, sneaking looks at me when she thought I wouldn't see. Soon she became the dog she was born to be — not a racing machine, but a loving, playful, silly, brilliant true friend! I named her Gypsy and she lived to be seventeen years old. She was the best friend I ever had. After she went to greyhound heaven, I adopted two more greyhounds in her honor, who are just as great in their own ways.

Believe it or not, Vic is still living out in the desert, saving dogs whenever he can. Every few months, he calls and tells me all the details. He says it often takes him a long time to catch one of these dogs, as they are pretty spooked after being dumped and starved for so long. He takes them to the humane society because he feels it would be unfair to his dogs to have more than six. He says that each of his dogs expects and deserves a certain amount of his attention every day, and that having more would be unfair. I can understand that logic. When I have more time and space, I would like to have a few more greyhounds myself. Meanwhile, I remain eternally grateful to my Uncle Vic for introducing me to these glorious desert dogs.

Mindy

Christin Ruge

Dogs lives are too short. . . their only fault, really.
— *A.S. Turnbull*

WE ADOPTED MINDY (her race name was Nita's Minnie) in
October, 1995. Mindy was a beautiful two-and-a-half-year-
old brindle greyhound. We decided to adopt a greyhound primarily to provide Max, our eight-year-old Springer spaniel,
with a companion.

Max and I went to a "greyhound fair" together. There is a
very active Greyhound Adoption Agency where we live in
Western Massachusetts. There are greyhound events monthly.
Interested families learn more about greyhounds and often
end up taking one of them home. As soon as I saw Mindy, I
knew she was the greyhound for our family. She was in a pen
with another greyhound. The two greyhounds behaved very
differently. Mindy was curious, moving around with her tail
wagging wildly, while the other greyhound was jumping and
barking. After taking her for a walk with Max and seeing that
they were compatible, I decided to give her a try.

The first few months with Mindy were a struggle. It was fun teaching her to go down the stairs. Once she learned she thought that was where her "bathroom" should be. She was extremely scared of all males, including my husband. In contrast, she became so attached to me that it was annoying. If I was in a room with the door closed, she was outside whining to get in. Every time I went into our attached garage, she would try to sneak out the door and jump into my car. Getting her out was almost impossible, since she resisted being pulled out and didn't listen to any commands.

Max, on the other hand, understands all commands we give him, although he sometimes takes his time following them. Not only is he smart, he has tremendous character. When we first got her, Mindy's primary characteristic was fear. She was scared that I was going to abandon her.

With a lot of love and patience, Mindy began to fit into our household. The first time Mindy walked over to my husband, Sean, and licked his face, it warmed my heart so much I got tears in my eyes. She is now so affectionate with Sean that he has nicknamed her the "Kissy Face Dog." Mindy also has so much character now that Sean gave her another nickname, "The Big Goofball Dog." Mindy has learned what the rules of the house are. She is now a very well-behaved lady.

Max did his part in welcoming Mindy too. He spends at least an hour every day licking her ears. Mindy and Max play together, hunt squirrels together, and bark at the mailman together. It's amazing how well they get along because they are completely opposite breeds and they behave very differently. Surprisingly, Mindy has learned a lot from Max.

When Mindy first started walking with Max she would hold her head high, alertly looking at everything around her. Because she is a "sight" hound, that is very natural for her. Max is a "scent" hound. He has his nose to the ground almost the entire time we are walking. I noticed after a couple of months that Mindy was doing the same thing. She was so curious about what Max was sniffing that she would follow him from bush to bush, sniffing everywhere he sniffed. I believe her curious nature is what saved her life.

Mindy had her biggest adventure on the windiest and coldest day in Massachusetts. I got home from work at around 3:30. As soon as I got in the door, I noticed that something was wrong. Mindy, who usually greets me at the door, wasn't there. I couldn't find her anywhere. I did, however, find a note on my dining room table from the police. The note read, "Your neighbor called us and reported the wind blew your doors open. Your greyhound got out and was hit by a car." Mindy was lost in the cold and injured!

Sean rushed home from work and we looked everywhere. I walked up and down every street in our neighborhood and the surrounding neighborhoods. Sean got in his car and drove around slowly, calling out her name. A neighbor called all the local vets and dog pounds. We have a very busy road outside of our neighborhood that I knew she couldn't have crossed especially during rush hour when the traffic is bumper to bumper. A humane officer told me that she was probably curled up somewhere trying to keep warm.

Nighttime was approaching and the temperature kept dropping. Sean and I were sick with worry. After it was dark, I went home, put on warmer clothes and went out again to look for Mindy. This time I took Max with me. We walked up and down every street. I thought that if she was out there and conscious, she would come to me if she heard my voice. I talked to all my neighbors and looked under their decks and in their sheds. Everyone was so helpful, but no Mindy.

Greyhounds are known for being unable to find their way home when lost. Now I was really afraid for Mindy. I knew she couldn't last the night in this cold weather. I left the garage door open with the light on and some blankets on the floor. I held out for a miracle, hoping that she would find her way home.

I went inside and made a dozen "Lost Dog" signs. I intended to put them in every gas station and convenience store around. As I opened the door into the garage, in came Mindy! My heart just about stopped. I immediately took her to the emergency room at the animal hospital. She had to wear a cast for awhile, but she was okay!

I believe that Mindy followed Max's fresh scent and that is how she found her way home. A couple of months earlier, I don't think she would have been able to find her way home. But she had a lot of practice sniffing after Max. Whatever the reason — she is alive.

Since her accident, she has become even more lovable. She is friendly to our guests now. She greets them at the door with her tail wagging. She is such a wonderful addition to our family. When she's curled up next to me in bed or on the couch, I often think about how we almost lost her. Then I remember just how lucky we are.

My Shayna

Greta Marsh

Reverence for life is the highest court of appeal.
— *Albert Schweitzer*

IT WAS A cold, cold day in the latter part of November, 1991, when the animal control officer received a frantic phone call. The caller advised that police had been summoned to shoot a "mad" dog in a local cemetery. The "mad" dog was a starving greyhound who was attempting to eat a dead cat through her racing muzzle. The animal control officer responded immediately and upon arriving at the cemetery she proceeded to chase the emaciated dog in order to keep her out of the clutches of the police, who were expected momentarily. After running for about a mile or more, the exhausted woman sat down on the tombstone to rest. Moments later the greyhound appeared and rested her head on the woman's lap. This special lady cared for the former racer for about a month, until there was room for the dog at Greyhound Friends in Hopkinton, Maine. According to the tattoo in one ear, she was four years old.

We visited Greyhound Friends on December 30, 1991, and that's how Shayna came into our lives. We named her Shayna because in Yiddish it means pretty and she sure is one elegant beauty. There are many sides to Shayna. Sometimes she's quiet, dignified and regal. Many persons therefore assume that our dog Murphy, who's part akita and part golden retriever, is the dominant one, but he's not. Shayna, who can be quite vocal and assertive, is. She's also a natural born comedian who likes to carry our shoes and boots from the mud room into the bedroom. She carries them in her mouth while looking straight ahead, avoiding any eye contact with us. Does she think we can't see her if she doesn't look at us? Once the footgear have been deposited in the bedroom, the fun begins. She throws them up in the air one after another like a juggler. But unlike a juggler, she doesn't catch them. they land on the floor with loud thuds and then she throws them up in the air over and over again. The fun continues for several minutes and once she's had enough she rubs her head against me for a minute or two and then settles down in her bed with a contented sigh. This elegant, graceful creature fills our lives with warmth, joy, laughter and love. It hurts to think about the many tens of thousands like her who are brutally murdered each year when they stop earning their keep. Dog racing must be stopped. It must be prevented from beginning in states where is not yet legal, and abolished wherever it's already established. I'm doing everything I can to see that it's abolished in Massachusetts.

Gracie

Hope Combest

If you pick up a starving dog and make him prosperous, he will not bite you. This is the principal difference between a dog and a man.
— *Mark Twain*

"SHE HAS A strong heart and the will to live." Those were the best words I had ever heard. Veterinarian Randy Jones was willing to take Gracie in and do whatever he could to help her. I couldn't believe it. Now it would be solely up to her. Did she really have a strong heart and the will to live? Only time would tell. That was three and a half years ago and today Gracie still has an enormous lust for life and continues to amaze everyone she meets.

Gracie's story begins on an April afternoon in 1992, when a frantic call came from a lady who had seen five greyhounds running loose near her home. She had tried to lure the greyhounds to come to her, but they were too spooked. It would now be up to us and Animal Control to catch these frightened dogs and bring them in to safety.

Two weeks passed and only one greyhound was captured in the live trap that had been set. The Humane Society took the large brindle male to the shelter only to euthanize him that same day because he was heartworm positive. Three of the greyhounds had died of starvation and only one remained alive but still uncatchable.

Perhaps she knew that we were only trying to help her or perhaps her hunger and her fear of the elements were stronger than her fear of people. Whatever it was, it drove her to come in and seek help. Fortunately, the lady who had originally called us had not given up trying to persuade the greyhound to come to her. To her surprise, she found the grey lying on her back porch early that April morning.

As soon as we received her call, we headed to Arlington to pick up "a very sick and hungry" greyhound. What we found when we arrived was horrifying.

The first time we laid eyes on Gracie we could barely stand to look at her. The tiny, frail, and bald body of a once glorious greyhound was now a mere skeleton barely weighing 30 pounds. During the time that she was running loose with the pack, she had been mauled severely. Her left eye was out of the socket, her entire head looked as though it was one solid laceration, and she was totally starved and dehydrated.

Unable to stand and walk on her own, Gracie was placed in my husband's arms and we left, truly believing she would die on the way to the vet. We decided to name her Gracie, because only by the grace of God would this precious life be able to continue.

Dr. Jones diagnosed Gracie with Sarcoptic mange and heartworms as well as very poor physical condition. As we had expected, she would be blind in her left eye. He said it would take several weeks to get her healthy enough to undergo the heartworm treatment, but he believed she had a strong heart and an even stronger will to live. It would be up to her to pull through this. It only took two weeks for Gracie's strength to build up and her blood count to normalize. She was ready to begin heartworm treatment and her Sacroptic mange was under control. She was really improving!

One week into the heartworm treatment, we noticed additional physical changes. Her upper abdominal area was expanding and our worst nightmare was about to unfold. Gracie was pregnant! Dr. Jones informed us that because of the cortisone treatment for the mange and the arsenic treatment for the heartworms, the puppies would either be stillborn or grossly deformed. She was due to whelp at any time.

On May 1, 1992 Gracie blessed our home with five beautiful brindle greyhound puppies. The three boys and two girls were all normal, all healthy and all greyhound! Even though the heartworm treatment prevented her from nursing, she was a super mom. She longed for her babies, but could only be with them for short periods of time and always chaperoned! In spite of this Gracie loved and nurtured her babies to the best of her abilities. Now only Gracie remains in Texas. As children will do, hers eventually moved away. Cheetara lives in Kentucky, Casey lives in Michigan, Airborne lives in North Carolina, and Freebie and Socks have passed away.

Today Gracie lives in a wonderful home in Texas. She has been there for three years and she shares her family's love with an Italian greyhound named Alex and a small terrier named Sam. She continues to fill her family's lives with love and devotion.

Greyhound Racing:
Misuse of God's Creation

Cheryl Lander

The greatness of a nation and its moral progress
can be judged by the way its animals are treated.
— *Gandhi*

IN THE SPRING of 1992 I had my first up close and personal
contact with an ex-racing greyhound. His racing name was
Houndini, but his foster parents, who were good friends of
mine, had renamed him Lance. They hoped to place him in a
home with patient and kind people because he would need
special attention to bring him out of the shell he had built
around himself while racing.

He was five years old, had very low self esteem, and had
little idea how to play with other dogs. He had lived in a cage
all of his life and so was quite frightened by the amount of
freedom in his new life. He was not fully housebroken, and it
was not known if he ever would be. He also was not used to
walking up or down stairs, and seemed to have little sense of

how large his body was. For example, he would try to turn around in a space that was much too small. He acted as if he was really not inside his body.

After my husband and I watched Lance run and play with our Airedale, Lizzie, and after looking into his big brown soulful and watchful eyes, we decided to adopt him. He joined our family in April of 1992. Now, more than four years later, Lance is still quite shy, but his playful side often comes out, especially when he runs up behind us and nips our butts. He is even learning to play with toys, give kisses, ask to go outside, and beg for Milkbones like the other dog. He still watches behind him for a quick path out of any situation, and he stares at us for hours in disbelief that he is free and loved.

We adopted Lance because we care for animals, we think that what is happening to racing greyhounds is unethical, and believe that protecting animals from such things is not only an ethical issue, but also a spiritual one. When I look into Lance's eyes, I feel sad about his life and the lives of so many like him.

Sixteen states in the USA currently have greyhound race tracks. It is not so much the racing itself that I oppose, for it is a wonderful sight to see these graceful dogs running; rather, it is the unnatural conditions that these dogs must endure (often living in a cage), and their uncertain future once they are no longer fast enough to win.

I agree with Gandhi, who said: "The greatness of a nation and its moral progress can be judged by the way its animals are treated."

In this country, we don't do a very good job of caring for our animals, just as we don't treat our children very well. In fact, recent studies link animal abuse with child abuse. I would go a step further and say that all abuse (e.g. child, animal, environmental) is linked to a single factor — our society has lost its ability to respect life, to see the sacredness in all life. Michael

Fox of the Humane Society says this: "The beauty, vitality, and wonder of the world are lost when nature is desacralized and exploited merely as a resource, and when animals are demeaned and treated merely as commodities, and when the creative process is controlled and directed to satisfy purely selfish ends without regard for the suffering of sentient life." (Fox, *Our Changing View of Animal Rights*)

Some of you might wonder whether animal exploitation is a spiritual or ethical issue. I say it is both. So do others, such as the great Russian novelist Fyodor Dostoevski: "Love all God's creatures, the whole universe and each grain of sand in it. Love every leaf, every ray of God's light. Love the animals. Love the plants, love everything. When you love every creature, you will understand the mystery of God in created things. Once you perceive it, you will begin to comprehend it better every day." (Fyodor Dostoevski, *The Brothers Karamazov*)

Saving animals from exploitation is a spiritual issue. I even believe that the call to action in Proverbs 21:8 encompasses the animal kingdom: "Open your mouth on behalf of the dumb, and for the rights of the destitute."

Just as Noah of the Old Testament did when he brought all the animals onto the ark before the flood, we must follow the command to preserve and care for all of God's creatures. When I look into the eyes of my greyhound, I am grateful for the opportunity to give a home to this beautiful animal and fellow creature of God. Through my relationship with this graceful and free creature, especially as I get lost looking into his eyes, I feel a connection to the rest of creation.

Beauty

Claudia Presto

Acquiring a dog may be the only opportunity
a human ever has to choose a relative.

— *M. Siegel*

She arrived late one Saturday night, after an eleven hour ride with a carload of six other greyhounds. All had been rescued from death and all were to be residents of the Greyhound Gang until they were healthy and happy. All of them would then go to loving homes.

She had no name, no known history and scars covered her tiny frame. She had been found wandering the streets of Tucson, lost, abandoned, unwanted. The Greyhound Gang had an adopter who wanted a small fawn female, so she was spayed one day and sent to us the next. She was ill, burning with a temperature of 105 degrees. By Sunday, she had claimed a corner of the couch as her own. I sat next to her, putting cold compresses on her feet to try to get the temperature down. I put baby food on my hand and she feebly licked it off. I syringed water down her throat. The small town vet was away hunting. I called Best Friends Animal Sanctuary, which was just up the road, and had a seasoned staff. I took her there and they put her on I.V. antibiotics and sent a blood sample to the lab. I spent all night Sunday watching, waiting, worrying that there was no significant change. Her ear tattoo told me she was five years old, her extended nipples told me that she had had a litter or two, her eyes told me she was in pain. I told her about the life that was waiting for her once she got well and the lady with the poodle who wanted to adopt a greyhound; she'd probably want to name her Precious, or Binky, or Tiffany. When I suggested Beauty, the greyhound looked deep into my eyes and put her paw on my arm. So Beauty it was. We limped along, Beauty still running a high temperature barely eating and drinking, until Tuesday. The blood test results arrived. Beauty had both immune affecting tick diseases, ehrlichiosis with a titer of 10,000 and babesiosis with a titer of 640. She was immediately put on a course of Tetracycline and within two days her temperature was back to normal, and she was off the couch. Within another week she was running and playing with the other dogs. within three weeks, she had replaced her coat with a new shinier, healthier one, and within a month, she had adopted me!

Beauty's days are now spent riding shotgun with me on all adoption trips, sleeping curled up on my bed with her head just touching the edge of my pillow, and chasing lizards amid the red rocks of southern Utah. What a beauty she is.

The Story of Ibiza

B. Anne Finch

Physical bravery is an instinct; moral bravery
is a much higher and truer courage.
— *Wendell Phillips*

I WENT ALONE for a week to the interesting old city of Salamanca
in Spain to take a course in the Spanish language for the purpose of aiding my work to help the greyhounds in Spain.
Salamanca was far away from the Mediterranean coast where
I had previously poked my nose into the tracks and kennels of
the greyhound stadiums. 1000 unfortunate greyhounds are
brought there each year from Ireland, to race their hearts out.
My relations with the tracks had deteriorated because the
Ministry of Agriculture sent my criticism to the directors of
the tracks. The directors, particularly at Valencia and Mallorca,
were furious, to such an extent that I was warned that it would
actually be dangerous for me to return.

Needless to say, my concern for the welfare of greyhounds
took me to the refuge outside of Salamanca. About 200 dogs

and cats and one baby fox were being tended there by several kind helpers, some of them doing social work instead of National Service. The animals were secure, and had regular meals. There was the usual flow of dogs and cats in and out during the course of the day. The kennels consisted of several concrete shelters within paddocks housing about five dogs. The dogs lie mainly on rough concrete and eat and drink out of communal troughs. They all looked well and happy but it was difficult to rid them of the ticks. A caretaker lived there permanently. There were several greyhound-like breeds but only one dog with an ear-mark who was pure greyhound. Her ear-mark was Spanish and she was painfully thin, her pelvic bones were protruding and her face appeared bumpy and bony under her thin skin. She was timid and gentle, and too polite and retiring to be able to cope with the battle for food among the five dogs. She limped because of a swollen foot, possibly caused by an old fracture, and she had an infected lump on her chest due to a pressure sore. She was white and black, with one of the most beautiful long tails I had ever seen. She seemed to expect nothing from anyone and stoically accepted her pathetic condition, having long ago given up any hope of affection and attention.

I couldn't get her out of my mind. The next day I went again, with towels for her to lie on and some antibiotic cream and bandages.

It was obvious that finding a home for her in Spain would be impossible. She had a chance in the U.K., Switzerland or Germany — but how could I get her there? If I had had a car and lots of money and time, it would have been so much easier. I had none of these things, and furthermore was I laden with a heavy suitcase of books and clothes and I was staying in a hostel without facilities.

I decided finally that she must come with me to Madrid.

To arrange export to England would be nigh impossible from Salamanca where there is no international airport. My aim was to get her to the island of Mallorca, to English kennels and friends I knew who could export her. But I didn't have a box for the air travel or the time to get there and back before my return flight to England, back to my nursing job. Export arrangements take a lot of time and trouble.

I decided to cancel my last day at the language school. I lost the money on my return bus fare to Madrid and instead hired a taxi which would take a dog — not an easy task in Spain. The journey from Salamanca to Madrid is about 150 miles and costs a fortune by taxi. I somehow had to find some kennels in Madrid. Sociedad de Protector de Animales in Salamanca had the same difficulty as I did trying to contact ANDA, the animal welfare society in Madrid. Neither of us could get an answer.

By chance, while walking around Madrid the previous weekend, I had seen a poster on a lamp-post with an address of another welfare society, not previously known to me or to the Sociedad's director at Salamanca. I tried them. They answered and then said I could bring the dog.

When I arrived, their office was closed for the siesta. I had one or two hours to kill with the dog and my suitcase, in a busy street in the heart of Madrid! I sought a cheap hostel in the neighborhood to dump my luggage. The idea of taking a dog into the hostel was met with utter astonishment, of course, and a refusal. I was most conspicuous in the center of Madrid with a skeleton-like greyhound. The taxi driver was an angel and although he couldn't comprehend what on earth I was about, he would not leave me alone with my problem. He even found a supermarket for me where we bought some tins of food for the dog which I could open without a tin-opener.

Eventually the office re-opened and I was welcomed in

such a way that I nearly burst into tears with relief. The last 24 hours had been a nightmare. Everything I tried to do had been met with a refusal and shrug of the shoulders, almost as if there was some pleasure to be gained in being able to refuse help. Someone in the office even spoke English, which was an enormous relief, and I overflowed with a torrent of words, able at last to express my feeling in my native tongue!

The dog, Ibiza ate well and silently closed her eyes in an upright position, not quite submissive or confident enough to lie down and not sure of what lay in store for her next. She wasn't used to security and affection and didn't yet know how to respond. I have seen this sort of "depression" in several greyhounds in England, where they were born and reared in kennels and used only as running machines for profit. This is why they are so often ignored in rescue kennels when people come to choose a pet. The same emotionless phenomenon exists in humans who have been deprived of love. In time, of course, with patience and constant kindness, they thaw and can respond in the normal way.

Ibiza was taken to kennels outside Madrid and promised a soft bed, good food, veterinary care and love. Upon my return to England I would set in motion plans for her future — was it to be England and six month quarantine? How could I pay for it? Or would it be Zurich or Germany? But how would I get her flown internally to Mallorca?

At 9:00 p.m., at the end of a long day, I needed my first bite of food. I found a bar that served "tapas" and began to tuck into a plate of "patatas fritas." Then I heard, from the overhead television the ubiquitous trumpet fanfare of bull-fighting in Sevilla. I watched a large black bull slowly topple, blood pouring from its spear-ridden shoulders as it fell dying on the sands of the arena, wet with rain and blood. It was difficult to swallow the next mouthful. In God's name, how is it that man can be so blind to the suffering of the innocent? How far have we really come in our civilization? Such cruelty and acts of neglect reflect our behavior as human beings and diminish us. And yet one must not forget the small devoted groups of people striving to turn the tide of evil to good. Even the taxi driver looked at Ibiza with emotion and called her a "santa."

Later, on my return to England, I heard of an English lady, in Alicante on the mainland, who would fetch Ibiza from Madrid and take her to her own kennels. The kennels in Madrid must have been very neglectful. She now had five ulcers and was very thin and miserable. The vet in Alicante said that four more days in those kennels and she would have died.

But now she was in safe hands. When she regained her strength, she was transported to England and went to quarantine kennels five minutes from my home where I could visit her regularly. At the end of her six month's confinement she found a home, with three whippets, and now lives in perfect bliss behaving like a puppy curling up together with her new little friends. She brings enormous joy to the family who so kindly offered her a home.

Her racing details (from the ear-mark) arrived from the Spanish Federation on the day of her fourth birthday. Her racing name was Taranta.

But we call her Santa.

The End of Posey Troubles' Troubles

Karen Harkin

> Cruelty to animals is one of the most significant vices
> of a low and ignoble people.
> — *Alexander von Humboldt*

POSEY TROUBLES HAS had more than her share of troubles in her six years of life. The bulk of this story — and it is sad — comes from bits and pieces gathered by people connected to her rescue. Had she been able to tell this herself, it would probably be worse than we surmise.

Not much is know about Posey before the fall of 1991. She was racing on a track in Wisconsin Dells, Wisconsin. At the end of the racing season, Posey became a pet for a young lady who worked at the racing kennel. This relationship was short lived as the girl soon obtained a job at an out-of-state track and could not take Posey with her. Posey was given to owner number two, a man who owned some rental cabins. Posey lived there only a few weeks and, as near we can tell,

46

was not happy. The man had several male dogs and Posey, who was not spayed at the time, probably opposed their advances. Posey went on to owner number three, a vacationing family from Illinois. The cabin owner did not give her away without conscience. He said that if they changed their minds and did not want the dog within the next two weeks, he would take her back. We judge that the family kept her for about two months. In early December 1991, the family contacted the previous owner in Wisconsin Dells and asked him to take Posey back. He was not interested since his two week "trial offer" had long since expired. This part of the story gets fuzzy as Posey "disappears" until January 23, 1992, when she was found by some young boys in a woods in Southern Illinois. The snow and bitter cold had taken its toll on her. Posey's 19 pound body was too weak to stand. Her beautiful black coat was brown-grey, patchy and crusty, full of cuts and scars. Her eyes must have still provided a glimmer of hope to these boys. They, and the people that follow, truly are her rescuers. One of the boys' father was a law enforcement officer. Upon seeing Posey, he immediately knew that if she were taken to the SPCA, she was destined to die. Instead they took her to Carole Krajeski, an angel sent from heaven to rescue abused animals. Although she was a groomer by trade, she had a reputation for mending sick and injured animals which were victims of cruel and in-humane abuse. She worked hard for weeks, with hourly feedings for Posey to get stronger. She nursed her wounds and made desperate attempts to find out who this dog was and why she had been made to suffer. Shortly, after receiving Posey, Carole tried to identify the dog through the National Greyhound Association. Due to the dehydrated condition of Posey's ears, Carole was unable to accurately read Posey's ear tattoos. The numbers Carole gave the NGA were for a dog that had already been destroyed. Because of the inability to identify her, she was nicknamed Emily Elizabeth by Carole's seven-year-old son, who immediately bonded with this dog. Emily Elizabeth (Posey) was regaining her strength and playing with the other canine residents of the house. However, she was aggressive towards the birds and cats, since just a few weeks before, creatures like these were probably her only meals. Soon Carole was able to read her tattoos and make a correct identification of Posey. NGA and Greyhound Pets of America did some research to find what little background information we now have. The Illinois family purposely left Posey in the woods in the coldest months of the year — unbelievable but true. We maintain that "their time will come," and Posey will have the final word with them.

By March of 1992, Posey was getting stronger and more aggressive. She weighed forty-seven pounds and was gaining everyday. It was time for her to move on. Through GPA, she was returned to Wisconsin, this time under the watchful eye of Dr. Rebecca McCracken. If there is a greyhound heaven, it must be at Dr. McCracken's house in Franksville, Wisconsin. There, Posey finished her healing and learned the fine art of being a house dog. She was spayed and had several vertebrae removed from her tail. Her tail, which had miraculously survived two months in the cold, could not handle the extreme abuse of hitting the wall during fits of happy wagging.

I obtained Posey in April 1992 and she has been a welcome addition to our family. Although she now weighs 67 pounds, she still bears the scars of her misfortunes on her legs. She no longer looks at birds and cats as something to eat but rather something to chase. During our time together, we have sampled many different canine disciplines — obedience, agility, lure coursing, but by far her favorite is just plain old walking. Late every evening, all year around, we walk the neighborhood streets. This is *her time* and she has earned it well.

In a letter written by Carole Krajeski when she sent Posey to Wisconsin, she summarized the ordeal of this poor dog: "Posey has been a small victory in a world of defeats." Posey's loving personality towards all people means that she must have forgiven all the human wrong-doing inflicted on her. We can only thank God and people like Carole and Dr. McCracken for providing Posey the opportunity to forgive her oppressors.

The Story of J.J.

Greta Marsh

Animals share with us the privilege of having a soul.
— *Pythagoras*

IT WAS 1984 and a trainer at a dog track in New England discovered that one of his racers was pregnant. She wasn't supposed to be, but she was. In April he brought her to a local veterinary clinic where she delivered her puppies. A veterinary technician who was present at the delivery adopted one of them and named him J.J. J.J. was a lucky greyhound; he never raced, was loved and well cared for. Then suddenly, J.J.'s good fortune changed.

In late February 1996, his guardian phoned me and explained that she was changing jobs and would be traveling throughout the U.S. and living in a trailer. She did not think J.J., who would soon be 12 years old, could survive such a lifestyle. I gave her the name and phone number of a local greyhound rescue/adoption group, suggested that she call the director, and then get back to me. A few days later she advised me that the rescue group was willing to take J.J., but he would be confined to a crate in a kennel until he was adopted. That could take as long as a year — or perhaps never — because not many persons want to adopt a senior citizen. The woman wept saying that J.J. would pine away and eventually die with this treatment. She felt it would be kinder to end his life with a lethal injection. That was totally unacceptable to me, so in March of 1996 J.J. entered our home and our lives.

I'm pretty certain that J.J. misses his original family, but he is sweet and loving, loves to play, and certainly does not fit the stereotype of a senior citizen.

My akita and former racing greyhound have accepted him well. Before leaving town, the woman's fiancé reminded me that J.J. could live another 3 months or another 3 years. I said I understood. J.J. will be 13 years old in a couple of weeks. He is teaching me how to live and appreciate one day at a time.

Bonnie and Pepper

Jane Marks

Animals cannot speak for themselves. . . cannot vote. . . so it is
incumbent on us to do as much as we can to ensure their freedom.
— *Dr. C. Kagan*

Four years ago I saw a news clip on the plight of the racing
greyhound. I thought for many months about what I had seen.
We have always had dogs, mostly Shelties, and we wondered
how anyone could possibly treat "man's best friend" with such
hatred. The following year I saw a documentary on television
about the predicament of the greyhound. This documentary
was even more disturbing than the news clip. I wrote down
the contact phone number, knowing I had to do something,
anything, to help at least one dog. We already had an older
dog, Pepper. Would he accept a new dog into a home that had
been exclusively his? I was not sure we had room for a second
dog, especially one as large as a greyhound. What was I think-
ing? All I knew was that I had to at least investigate the possi-

Unable to stand
on sore feet,
caged Masay
awaits a race.

Anne Finch

Masay after
being rehabilitated

Stubby

Kim Owens

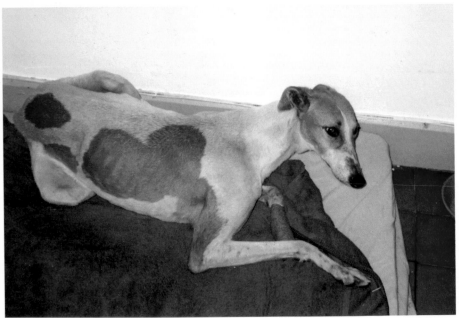

Demi when rescued

Melanie Sharp Bolster

Susie
(happy girl
now)

Bobby Wolner

Demi
after
being
cared
for

Jill Hopfenbeck

Shayna

Greta Marsh

Gracie

Hope Combest

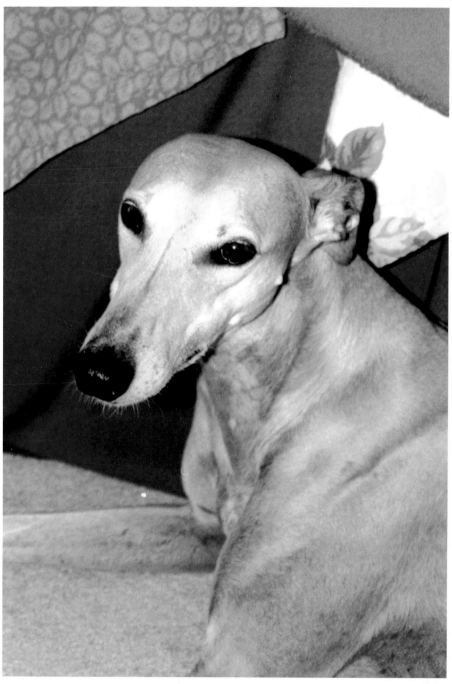

Beauty   *Claudia Presto*

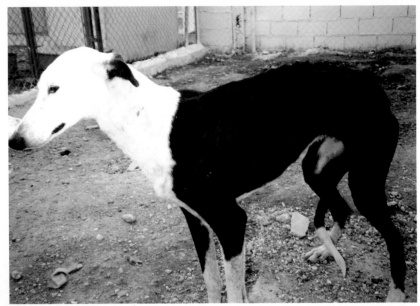

Ibiza when rescued

Ibiza now cared for

Anne Finch

Posey

Karen Harkin

J.J. sniffing the air on the first day of spring

Greta Marsh

Boston Boy   *Louise Coleman*

Outlaw (Zowie)   *Kari Mastrocola*

Sadie and Manny   *Bruce Meier*

Mark   *Bill Roth*

Morningstar   *Bee Lint*

Oso Special trying on his Christmas sweater   *Nora Star*

Angie settling in for a nap

Alexis Rippe

Lauren & Dan Emery

Bernie &
Boomer

Gator and the Governor   *Scotti Devens*

Thumper and Emeril   *Kevin Barber*

Sandy   *Pat Burton*

Indie and her two surviving pups   Pat Burton

Jodi-May relaxing   Nora Star

One of the dogs rescued with Outlaw (Zowie) and
rehabilitated at the Tucson Humane Society

*Be comforted, little dog.
Thou too at the
resurrection shall have
a golden tail.*

Martin Luther

bilities. So I made the call. I spoke with Susan Netboy, the founder of Greyhound Friends for Life, who told me about the temperament and needs of the greyhound. Everything I heard sounded almost too good to be true. Susan put me in contact with Nora Star and arranged to visit. After a few minutes into the visit, I was totally and helplessly in love. The female, Bonnie, was the gentlest, sweetest dog I had ever had the pleasure to meet. She looked like a fawn. She had huge brown eyes, a big black nose and the most innocent expression one can imagine. Bonnie did, however, have a physical problem. Two of her hind toes had been amputated, but she seemed to get around just fine. The other greyhound, Marco, was a few inches taller than Bonnie and just as beautiful. My heart gravitated to Bonnie, even though she had a foot problem and was very thin. I knew that she would make a wonderful addition to our family. I made arrangements to bring her home with me the next day. I was hoping and praying all the way home that Pepper would be as happy with his new "sister" as I was. I could not have made a better choice! Pepper and Bonnie bonded almost instantly. Pepper enjoyed having Bonnie to keep him company when we were away at work. They walked together beautifully, just as if they had grown up together. Pepper remained our alpha dog, even though Bonnie made two of him in size.

Pepper passed away last year, leaving a huge hole in our family. We adopted a Sheltie, Cassie, who had been abused and was found abandoned in the streets of San Francisco. Cassie now runs underneath Bonnie's legs and nips at her heels when she wants to play. Bonnie is still the same gentle, affectionate "fawn" I fell in love with three years ago, and has now assumed the role of alpha dog. Both dogs are "house" dogs, preferring to be with the rest of the family at all times. It is constantly play time with Bonnie and Cassie.

They keep the family entertained and laughing. The love we give these two comes back a million fold every day we are together. All they require is feeding, walking and a little love. Life could not be any better.

Boston Boy

Louise Coleman

Search and see if there is not some place
where you may invest your humanity.
— *Albert Schweitzer*

I REMEMBER WHEN he had to die — an old sweet dog sick with cancer. He clung to his bed and hated to go anywhere. Dr. Jill Hopfenbeck came and gave him an injection and sent him to heaven. We both cried.

Boston Boy was a seasoned racer, aged five, when I got him. I hadn't thought about getting a dog. It just seemed too bad that a dog with a name like Boston Boy was going to be destroyed and would get no reward for all his work. An extraordinary racer, he finished at five at a top track and was never graded off.

After I brought him home and tried to introduce people to him, he would act like a canine statue. I nicknamed him Shadow because he shadowed me. But alone with my son Nolan and I, he was demonstrative and himself.

Shadow wasn't alone for long. He became long-suffering and patient as more greyhounds entered and passed through his home. Trainers, who knew about his adoption kept calling up to ask me to find homes for more dogs. Greyhounds sat on all the couches and chairs. Boston Boy was permanent; he knew that he was for keeps, for good. But he was like a stone thrown into still water. From him concentric circles started. They are still going out. He had a good dog's soul; he was the sweetest boy. Through Shadow my bond with greyhounds was formed.

By the simple act of sparing one dog his death, my life was altered. Many people and circumstances remained the same, but the connections became much more intense, varied and extensive. I never would have circled out so far had I not brought Shadow home that day. Exhausting work pushes the ripples out, and help comes. My life changed on Mother's Day, 1983, the day Shadow came. Many people hope for a definitive moment to galvanize their lives. My moment came and brought Boston Boy. He was a real gentleman, my ever loving and faithful Shadow.

The Transformation
of an Outlaw

Kari Mastrocola

> Perseverance is not a long race...
> it is many short races one after another.
>
> — *Anonymous*

I GREW UP with greyhounds, in fact, many animals, both domestic and wild, were taken in throughout my childhood. Some
of the non-domestic animals had been abused and I formed a
very special relationship with them. I started showing dogs
when I was seven and I was one of the top junior handlers in
the nation during that career. I went to work for a top greyhound kennel in England, and I worked for a sighthound kennel
in Australia. I was active in the dog-show judging in the AKC,
and all this began my interest in animals. Five years ago I became active in greyhound rescue in northern California. On
one of my first days volunteering with this organization, I fell
in love with one of the greyhounds and hoped to have him
for my own. Zowie's story (formerly Outlaw) became a fa-

57

mous case. It was the beginning of one of the most difficult yet enriching chapters in my life. His story is one of many well deserving greyhound stories we would like to pay tribute to in this book. Maybe the book can be a reminder that not only is there injustice and pain in the world, but with concentrated effort, we can all do our part to make it better.

On my first day of helping with the rescue, I was to help socialize the greyhounds. I had two that I was to lead train and take out into the world, a world far removed from the racing world they knew. Outlaw came out of the crate and the bond was instant. It was love at first sight when we made eye contact. He truly has the most expressive eyes I have ever seen. I believe that the gentle, sensitive, spiritual nature of these animals is inherent, but the experience they have been through touches me even more deeply and makes them that much more special. We have so much to learn from these gentle creatures.

Zowie was to be adopted out that same afternoon but I knew that I had to have him. My mind was preoccupied with thoughts and feelings about Zowie going into a home other than mine. Later that afternoon I called the rescue group, and asked if he was gone. They told me it was not a good match with the people who had planned to adopt him. We then negotiated the best situation for everyone involved. I was in the process of moving and I resigned myself to sleeping in my car if I had to, in order to have this dog. They kept Zowie for a couple of months until I was settled. I drove to visit regularly, sometimes twice a day, to see my Zowie. It was not until later that I learned of his background. He seemed to have won the hearts of many.

Zowie, Outlaw at the time, was part of a well known legal case. One hundred dogs had been left to starve to death when their racing careers were over. Only about half of these dogs survived. I saw newspaper articles about Zowie that showed him at about 25 pounds, his normal weight being 70 pounds. He also spent one year in the Tucson Humane Society as evidence in the court case.

Zowie has been my constant companion now for five years. He has appeared on television numerous times and on the front page of the San Francisco Chronicle. He has also been featured in the "Celebrating Greyhounds" calendar in both 1996 and 1997. Approximately a year and a half ago he was diagnosed with Ehrlichia, a disease from the brown dog tick. He had most likely gotten it in Arizona from the tick-infested kennel where he raced, and it lay dormant in his system for four years. He was quite sick for a year and once it had progressed to the most severe stage symptoms appeared. I am happy to report that he is well and acting more and more like a puppy each day, even at the age of nine.

Zowie is one of the fortunate ones to have survived, and I am even more fortunate and blessed to have him as part of my life. We are inseparable!

Alex

Claudia Presto

I am in favor of animal rights as well as human rights.
That is the way of a whole human being.
— *Abraham Lincoln*

ALEX NEVER REALLY had a chance. He was a spook. He was
frightened of his own shadow, of people, of the track, of other
dogs, of everything. He would cower in the back of his crate
at the kennel and only come out if the door was left open and
if his handlers moved far away and turned their backs.

Getting him on the track to run wasn't even a consideration. Greyhound Adoption League of Tucson would just shake
their heads. What could they do? He wouldn't race, and how
would they get him adopted when they could barely get him
out of his crate?

The difficult decision was made. Alex had to be put to
sleep. He'd been in the adoption kennel for over 3 months
with no change is sight, and there were other greyhounds
needing his chance. So it was decided, "Take him to the vet,

it's time." Two weeks later Alex was still in his crate. I couldn't do it," was the response.

It was no life for him cowering all day long. So the decision was made again. Two weeks afterwards Alex was still there. "I think we'll have to tranquilize him first, then take him to the vet," was the decision. Again, no one could do it. Alex continued to live a shrinking shadow in his crate.

Linda Brown of Retired Racers, Inc., in Acton, California, heard of Alex from GAL. "I'll give him a try," she said gallantly. After over 6 months in GAL's adoption kennel, Alex was given another chance and he was brought to Linda's adoption facility.

Alex didn't change his ways at Linda's. She thought, "Maybe he'll like the house." But he didn't, so he was given his own clubroom in the kennel, complete with sofa and dog door. He eventually accepted Linda somewhat, and her daughter, but that was it; no one else could get near him. A year passed. Many adopters visited Retired Racers, Inc., but none went home with Alex. Most never even got a look at him.

Then one day a woman from Beverly Hills appeared. She had already agreed to adopt a little blue female along with the shy mixed breed she'd rescued when he'd been thrown out of a car. Linda mentioned Alex to her. She went into Alex's clubhouse and reappeared two hours later with Alex. "I'll take him, too," she said.

The first night, in his 8000 square foot home in Beverly Hills, Alex went right up to the bedroom with the owners and the other dogs. He surveyed the variety of beds, and with an impervious air, chose the leather chaise lounge as his. Alex was home.

Freedom

Gary Stahl

My new dog's name is "Freedom,"
yet times it did not know,
for it went by another name
in the past not long ago.

Her old name was much different,
one not of her own,
given to her by the master
like a slave . . .
. . . isolated
. . . alone

"Better Be Good," the announcer would say
as my dog lined up
forced into racing.
Chase the lure . . .
. . . win the cup

Yet scars show how difficultly
the losses tallied up,
for my graceful dog
at the end just didn't have enough.

"Freedom suppressed and again regained,"
so Cicero might say.
Glory be to "Friends for Life"
and to all the greyhounds . . .
freedom gained.

Sadie and Manny

Bruce Meier

> Old age means realizing you will never
> have all the dogs you wanted to.
>
> — *Joe Gores*

OUR FIRST UP-CLOSE ENCOUNTER with a greyhound was on a trip to the great northwest several years ago. About ten minutes into a visit with some friends in Portland we noticed what, at a quick glance from the next room, appeared to be a statue. There, lying peacefully on the other side of the dining room table, was Rosie. Her owners called her into the living room. We gazed at this amazingly sleek, calm, affectionate, three-year-old female striding gracefully up to us to win our hearts almost immediately. Her exotic tan and black brindle coloring, beautiful soft coat and loving demeanor made us want "a Rosie of our own." As if by design, our friends arranged for us to meet the director of a greyhound adoption agency who happened to live only blocks away. There we met two more greyhounds and saw photos of others. The director must have known we were falling in love with this magnificent breed. She took information and notes about us and our living situation, and then we were on our way. We continued up into Washington and British Columbia, enjoying thoroughly the rest of our three week trip. We returned home to the San Francisco Bay Area on a Sunday and received a call the very next day. There was a greyhound female for us if we wanted her. We did not hesitate one second. Again, as if by design, we had an associate who happened to be flying into San Francisco the next day from Portland, and *voila!* After a few phone calls it was arranged. We were *so* excited that night, like kids waiting for Santa on Christmas Eve.

The next day at the airport we paced in anxious anticipation at the Special Baggage claim area. We were behaving not unlike expectant parents about to adopt a child. We were adding a new member to our *pack!* Before we saw her, there were little nagging questions. Do we have enough time to spend with her? Would she...? What if...? All that was quieted when the roll-top metal door loudly rattled open in front of us. The crate appeared and out poked a very black shiny nose! We pulled the door up, and out she stepped. What a pretty face and athletic body. She was obviously just recently retired and in great shape. A hot-pink collar scintillated against her brilliant black coat; there was a white blaze on her chest. She did a little gyrating shake and dance. Alert eyes, ears and snout surveyed the landscape as if to say, "So this is San Francisco? Okay, let's go!" She was so cool and collected. Then she saw our friend (with whom she had flown). She jumped up on him as if to say, "Thanks, this is great!" She was attracting lots of smiles and got a few friendly pats as we proudly strutted through the terminal. It was suddenly a different, much more joyful world for us.

After adopting Sadie, we were concerned about her being alone hours at a time. We inquired about who might be available locally. We saw so many gorgeous dogs waiting for adoption. One in particular stood out. He had the same coloring as Sadie — a shining black coat with a white blaze on his chest. His name was "My Mannigan," and what a handsome five-year-old boy he was. We decided instantly on this dog and Manny is a proud addition to our family. He is strong, handsome, very spirited and loyal, extremely affectionate; and he has been a good guard dog for us too. Sadie accepted him eagerly. She has shown him the ropes to stair climbing, getting in and out of the car, which sofas are okay to lie on, etc. Our greyhounds have added untold happiness to our lives! We are always informing people who ask — every time we go out in public — what great pets, companions and friends they make!

Life With Mark

Bill Roth

> Amid all the forms of life that surround us, not one,
> excepting the dog, has made an alliance with us.
> — *Maurice Maeterdinck*

I PROMISED MY KIDS three years ago that when we bought a
new house with a large yard we would get a dog. The time
had come to honor my promise.

One day we saw a sign outside a local pet supply store
advertising a display of greyhound dogs for adoption. At first
we were hesitant because we didn't want a large dog. My wife
thought that greyhounds were kind of ugly and expected them
to be hyperactive since they are used to running 50 miles per
hour. Our kids insisted on stopping to look at the dogs anyway.

What a surprise! Most of the dogs were lying down as if
they were on valium or something; they had those big brown
eyes staring and saying "how about a hug?" They weren't ugly
at all. As a matter of fact, they had a deer-like quality and a

grace and beauty that was astounding! Then we looked at the list of characteristics. This might be the dog from heaven, everything we had dreamed of. They do not smell, they are not aggressive, and to top it off, it costs only $150 to adopt one. Someone had to be kidding us — this couldn't all be true! After talking to the people who brought the dogs and lived with them, they had us pretty well convinced to fill out an application, and afterwards, go out to a foster home to have a look at some of the available dogs.

Several weeks later we received a call from Barbara, who kennels several dogs. She said we should come and have a look. My wife and I told the kids, "Now we are only going out to look at these dogs, we are *not* bringing one home." To make sure of this we took the Honda, which barely held us.

When we got to Barbara's house I thought that we had been duped into believing these were not hyper or aggressive dogs. "Look at them, they're wearing muzzles, and they are jumping all over the place." Barbara just laughed and said, "Oh, they are only wearing muzzles to keep from biting each other when they play, and they're jumping around because they're so happy to see people, and they're craving your attention." I felt guilty for reacting so negatively. Barbara opened the gate to the kennel and several of the dogs came out to greet us. One fawn colored dog in particular struck our fancy. He came over to my wife and put his head in her lap. He looked up at her with those big brown eyes and said "Take me home.""Oh, that's Mark," Barbara said, "He's one of my favorites." We were hooked! We couldn't leave without this dog. Now what could we do? We didn't even have a car big enough to take him home. The kids begged us, saying that they would lie on the floor in order to take him home. After expert instructions from Barbara on how to begin our new life with a greyhound, we loaded him in the car and yes, the kids had to practically lie on the floor in order to fit him in. He was absolutely petrified by the experience. Loading a large dog with stiff frightened legs into a small car is quite an experience, but with a little coaxing, some doggy treats, and four people pushing and pulling, we finally got him in the car.

We arrived home, but without a crate, because the trunk of a Honda is not nearly large enough. We found a local pet store that had the size crate we needed and purchased it that day so that Mark would have a place to sleep for the next two weeks until he could be housebroken.

Since it was Mark's first experience inside a home, some rather strange events took place. He kept walking into walls and trying to go out sliding glass doors without opening them first. He would not go up the stairs. The first time we let him out of his crate, we immediately let him into the house without letting him out first, so he lifted his leg on my wife's favorite wingback chair in the living room. After reading several chapters of "Adopting the Racing Greyhound," we soon learned the proper way to handle these situations, and after a few days Mark was comfortable with his new surroundings. He was rather shy at first, and did not seem to have much of a personality. As time went on, he grew quite fond of us, and now has quite a personality. He gets very excited when we come home at the end of the day. I don't know why that tail doesn't break from wagging so violently. Now the mention of the word "car" starts that tail wagging, and going for a walk is like winning the lottery for him!

Everything we were told is true. The greyhound ideal characteristics are absolutely perfect for our needs. My yard still looks beautiful. When you walk into our house, you can't tell we have a dog. Our neighbors are not aware of the dog because he barks only when he hears our car drive up. He isn't aggressive when people come over. He loves little children.

Half of the time, our guests don't even know he is around because after a few minutes of getting to know them, he goes upstairs and lies in his favorite place, my daughter's bed.

We can not imagine life without Mark now. When I am away on a business trip, the kids put the phone receiver to his ear so that I can talk to him and they claim he wags his tail when he hears my voice. We take him to a local enclosed park where he puts on quite a show for everyone, running at top speed for several minutes, and then finishing up his exercise by lying down in complete exhaustion, waiting for other dogs to finally catch up with him. It's so funny to watch other dogs try to catch him when he is running! A greyhound moving at full speed is incredibly beautiful. The grace and speed have to be seen to be believed.

A month ago I went on a business trip to Phoenix, and out of curiosity I went to a local greyhound track to see what the races are like. I have to admit, it was exciting seeing up to 15 dogs running at full speed for a prize they could never reach. I was saddened though, when I began to think about what would happen to all of those incredible animals when their jobs at the track come to an end. That sadness soon turned to elation when I realized I would be going home in a few days to my dog Mark. He will be jumping up and down, licking me and wagging the incredibly long tail, happy to know that he now gets to run because he loves to, and not because he has to.

The Greyhound's Flight
Bee Lint, Pawnee

The greyhounds are sacred and centuries old
Their fight for life in truth must be told
The demon of our greyhounds is their masters' greed
Your racetrack of hell as their flight proceeds
Our greyhounds life you put on hold
Their worn-out bodies just four years old
The greyhounds' flight breaks its masters mold
Doomed for experimentation, left out in the cold
Those with greed think they have no soul

The greyhounds' flight will reflect the evil
    that dwells in the folds
Our work, our letters will keep flooding in
Our love of our greyhounds will win in the end

Dedicated to my beloved Tara
rescued by Greyhound Friends for Life

Oso Special's Therapy

Nora Star

> To the really ethical person, all of life is sacred, including forms of life
> that from the human point of view may seem lower than ours.
> — *Albert Schweitzer*

I ENJOY HELPING greyhounds in whatever way I am able, but I like most the hands-on care of fostering dogs who are waiting for their new homes. Although similar in many ways, each dog has a definite air of individuality. I usually choose the dogs who need lots of attention to make the transition. Susie (see *Susie's Story*) sat in the back of a closet shaking for weeks. She was probably the most severely traumatized greyhound I fostered. Lance (see *Greyhound Racing: Misuse of God's Creation*) was a close second.

A small black female named Sprite was third. When she arrived she sat on the blanket I put down for her and shook and froze there. My beagles enjoyed being my assistants in this fostering project. They decided to bring all their favorite toys and offer them to this terrified dog. In only a few minutes,

Sprite responded and began investigating the various treasures offered her. It was safer to respond to another dog than to a human. They coaxed her into going out the back door and touring the yard with them, and soon socialization began.

In time, of course, I had to keep a few of these dogs for myself. It was very satisfying seeing them go off to their new homes, but a part of me always went with them, and I knew that one day I would have to adopt. My first adoption was Jodi-May, a brindle female who I have had for four years and who is still somewhat wary. Two years ago I added a male to my family, a fawn named Oso Special. He is a rowdy extrovert who loves nothing more than giving and receiving affection. Total strangers have offered to buy him from me. *No sale.* He is a very important part of our family now.

Oso seemed to have more energy than the other dogs so I thought a second career (now that racing was over) might be fun for him. We tried pet therapy at a local convalescent hospital. The first time we visited it took him about five minutes to evaluate the environment and figure out what his role would be. It was, of course, what he does best — giving and receiving affection and love! Most of the residents are in wheelchairs and they gather in the TV room to see him. He is very sensitive and seems to sense which people to be a little distant with, and who wants a kiss on the cheek. The residents know him by name, know of his racing background and have his pictures up on their bulletin board. they look forward to his visits and talk about him between these visits. One day the nurse took me aside and told me that Oso Special is the only visitor some of the people have, and certainly the only kiss some of them ever get.

Oso looks forward to these visits as much as the residents do, and he seems to know how revered he is by these senior citizens.

Alaska Angie

Alexis Rippe

The one absolutely unselfish friend that a person can have in this
selfish world, the one that never deserts him, the one that never proves
ungrateful or treacherous, is his dog.

— *George Vest*

IT'S A BEAUTIFUL day. The rain has ceased, at least for the moment. Angie and I are passing the park on our daily jaunt
when a young child approaches. He has been feeding bread
to the ducks and now commences to feed it to Angie. He
asks why I have a tiger-striped baby deer on a leash, and
why her fur is so soft. I quietly explain that Angie is a greyhound dog who used to race in Florida. Her color is brindle,
the usual greyhound color. Meanwhile, Angie is enjoying
the bread, taking each piece gently and planting large greyhound kisses on the little boy's hand. In a few minutes the
boy runs back to his mom, loudly announcing that he had
just met a *real* race dog.

That is life with Angie now. The road to her emergence as

a wonderful companion took two and a half years to travel and had many a crevasse. She was the greyhound from Hell.

Her arrival in Juneau was one of those blessings in disguise. I was in the process of packing the car for a three week trip through Washington and western Canada, which included an obedience camp and several shows. It was not the best time to receive a new member of the family. However, arrive she did, late on a Sunday evening, courtesy of Mark Air and the Ketchikan dog pound.

When I first saw Angie, she was lying quietly in her airline crate with an expressionless face. She willingly accepted the sighthound walking lead, and off to the car we went. After meeting the other seven members of the household we all came inside. I showed her around. After her tour, she went to her quilt and just stood. Two hours later she finally curled up on the quilt.

The next day, after a quick visit to the vet, we left on our trip. I have been told greyhounds love to travel. Not this one. She hated the ferry. I had to carry her on and off at each stop. She hated the car, and tried a heart-stopping escape in the middle of the Kootenay National Forest. She decided to return to me as I sat on a rock beside a creek, wondering how to find her or if she would ever come back. We had a long talk and I think she began to realize that she was stuck with me, the car, and the rest of the trip.

At a show in Spokane, I was set up next to another whippet exhibitor, who was quite interested in my greyhound. Ironically, it was one of the Spokane area rescue people. I spent some time talking with her and it was there I discovered why Angie attacked my whippet, snarled at having her feet touched and would not allow anyone or anything near her food. You guessed it — I have an alpha greyhound. The Spokane rescue people provided me with their new owner information as well as a plastic, all weather muzzle. The muzzle proved to be the key to Angie's survival and her transformation into what she is today.

Once we were back home I started to piece together Angie's past. I searched for the best method of handling the extreme dominance that she displayed, which is not at all typical of greyhounds. Over the span of several months the story was revealed. She was adopted by a Ketchikan resident who loved her but could not bond with her. Shortly after arriving from Florida, Angie escaped. Her race led her to the ferry terminal and up onto the tie-down areas. Eventually she jumped over a barrier and into the frigid water. The ferry crew of the M/V Matanuska saw her jump and lowered a lifeboat, caught her collar with a gaff hook and pulled her unconscious body into the boat. She was reunited with her owner via a phone number and adoption number on her collar.

Now Angie not only owed her life to the adoption people but also to the Alaska Marine Highway System. That incident explained why she hated the ferry on our trip. In April, five months after arriving in Ketchikan, her adoptive family decided she needed a different home and they tried to place her locally. She was surrendered to the Ketchikan dog pound. I learned of her existence then, but I was assured that she was adopted. I left my name and phone number with them anyway.

Apparently, in Angie's second adoptive environment, she was kept in the car most of the time. (No wonder she hated the car.) She was left in situations where she was found roaming the streets. She was again surrendered for adoption. On Sunday, May 10, 1992, at the great cost of $5, she was adopted for the last time and flown to me in Juneau.

After her arrival, I discovered the phone number and adoption number on her collar. Again, that phone number was to be her salvation. I contacted the adoption agency and spoke to the director. I let him know that I now had Angie. He was very upset at her circumstances, but agreed to let me keep her. He changed all of her records into my name and arranged for me to receive all of the adoptive owner information.

After our return from the "trip from Hell with the dog from Hell" I phoned the adoption people with the list of Angie's problems and behaviors. That call began a lasting relationship with the organization. Over the course of the next two years they provided me with Angie's kennel evaluation, which described her as playful, not a fence fighter, and a bit afraid of the leash. They also stressed that, if at any time working with her became too much, they would gladly welcome her back into the program. They provided a wealth of information on behavior, training, and insights on working with greyhounds in general. They truly wanted Angie to succeed, and without their encouragement and help I probably would have given up.

Relaxation was a big problem for Angie. I worked with the Tellington Touch method, and got her accustomed to being touched everywhere, including her feet. Two and a half years later I could finally clip her toenails.

Slowly increasing dominant postures and behavior on my part helped her learn who the pack leader was. She does not sleep on my bed, but in her own on the floor right next to mine. I can reach out and cover her when she gets cold. She can also reach up and lick my hand. She is my alarm clock. There is no sleeping through Angie!

I spent almost a year building positive experiences around her food bowl. The reward for that occurred on the day I put the wrong thyroid pills into her bowl and, while she was eating, I just reached in and scooped them out. She never missed a mouthful.

Her fear of the car was cured by taking her for rides in the car with increasing frequency. The ride always included something that was fun to do — a romp in the park, or buying a hot dog and feeding it to her.

Angie was also trained in basic obedience. She has cataracts and doesn't see the jumps very well, so she will never compete in trials. The more confidence she gathered, the more her behavior improved, and that was the payoff.

She still goes into race mode in the yard, so the muzzle is in place whenever she is out in the yard running free. Consequently there have been no more attacks on my other dogs.

Her best buddy is Java, one of my Italian greyhounds. He can do anything to her and get away with it. Her running buddies are Curry, a larger whippet, and Caboose, a small French bulldog. They are a hilarious sight to behold!

Angie has mastered the art of digging, courtesy of the fifteen-year-old Siberian, and she has tutored Curry and Caboose in this skill. Together they are digging a passage to China.

She is the comedian of the back yard and the neighborhood celebrity. Angie has become a sweet, loving, and definitely playful greyhound. She also now loves her leash.

In September of 1995, we flew to Philadelphia to attend a greyhound reunion picnic. It was an overwhelming experience to see over 500 greyhounds in one place, all getting along.

Taking a very small part in the rescue of a greyhound named Angie has been an incredible experience for me and one that I will never regret.

Passing the Gator Bill

Scotti Devens

It is the sheer vulnerability and powerlessness
of animals, and correspondingly our absolute
power , over them which strengthens and compels
the response of more generosity.
— *Professor Andrew Linzey*

GATOR IS A handsome, striking, sleek greyhound. He used to
race at a track in New Hampshire. His life was a very unhappy
one, as I think it is for practically every greyhound that races.
I adopted him through a New Hamphire adoption agency in
June of 1991, unaware of the real issues of greyhound racing
dogs and their suffering. Immediately upon learning the ap-
palling truths about this industry and how these dogs are treated,
I realized that my role was clearly defined: greyhound racing
had to stop in the state of Vermont, at least as a beginning.

Using the process of petitions and working with legislators who were sympathetic to our cause, our organization, called *Save the Greyhound Dogs! Inc.* was able to find sponsors for our bill, SB152. This bill was named the "Gator Bill," in honor of my wonderful dog who, in coming into my life, caused me to learn of suffering that I had never conceived was possible.

A minimum of three days a week was spent at the Statehouse talking with and educating all parties. Every one of them was shocked and appalled when presented with documented information on the suffering of these gentle animals.

This bill was passed by the first senate committee unanimously. It was also passed unanimously by the Senate, and close to unanimously by the House.

It should be noted that Vermont took a very significant step when our wonderful governor, Howard S. Dean, M.D. signed this bill into law. In the spring of 1995 Vermont became the very first state in the country to prohibit and ban greyhound racing, simulcasting, and pari-mutuel betting.

It was a happy day indeed for greyhound dogs in the state of Vermont, but there is much work left to be done. This was barely the beginning.

Thumper and Emeril

Kevin Barber

> There are two ways of spreading light:
> to be the candle. . . or to be the mirror that reflects it.
> — *Edith Wharton*

THEY SAY when true love happens you can't deny it — even if
the girl has a kid, you have to take them both; it just happened
that the girl's kid was a six-year-old greyhound.

There was chemistry from the first moment between
Rebecca and me. My first glance at Thumper evoked a series
of predictable questions, the same question I would later hear
a thousand times on virtually every walk. "What kind of dog
is that. . . Oh yeah, is she fast?" I could have sworn I saw them
both wince.

Thumper was two months fresh off the track; she'd done
well and had been very pampered. Although both females were
very independent, Thumper leaned toward the timid side. Se
wasn't very comfortable with men and if I looked at her wrong
it seemed like she'd almost cry. How could I have known I'd

become a step-dad to a greyhound? I should have known I was in trouble when half of the pictures on every roll of film Rebecca took were of Thumper. Also, Rebecca couldn't stop talking about that dog.

Thumper was a rescued dog. I had never heard of such a thing. I knew that they raced but I knew nothing of the people that raced them or even where to find a track. I knew nothing about the number of beautiful, gentle comedic animals like Thumper that were being killed by the thousands every year. The more I learned the more I fell in love with the breed, with Thumper and with Rebecca too.

I live in Los Angeles and flew up to the Bay Area once or twice a month for almost a year before finally moving in and really getting to know Thumper. Except for a little chewing (some of which I'm sure she does on purpose) she's been great. She and I go on walks together. It was now my turn to field the questions over and over again from wide-eyed people thrilled to be this close to a real greyhound. "One time I rode on one to Sacramento," a kid laughed. Once, after being asked for the thousandth time what she was, I told a woman that Thumper was a sloth. She bought it. I almost feel bad now.

I feed her biscuits and we take naps together; of course hers last about twenty hours longer than mine. Things are going nicely. She let her guard down a bit and I took full advantage of it.

Having grown up around dogs, I know something about their behavior. One big part of a dog's life is playing, and Thumper didn't know how. How could this be? I learned that the life of a racing greyhound has no tennis balls, no stuffed toys, no room to play; just a cement run, a crate, and a track. Imagine. So being the only other 'dog' in our pack, I taught her how to play. Romping in circles on the floor is a favorite. She plays catch with a tennis ball — not actually catching it or bringing it back but chasing it till it stops. She sniffs at it, then at top speed runs straight at me with a big greyhound smile on her face. Sometimes I think I get more exercise when we play catch than she does.

I soon learned that this dog was a comedian. She was rolling over, walking through the house with her tongue sticking out the side of her mouth, dancing at even the mention of the word "walk." We spell it out now when we talk. "Honey, did you want to take Thumper for a w-a-l-k?"

It also appears that she carries a particular towel or toy for specific times of the day and certain rooms. Thumper even cleans up her towels and toys before going to bed! What a lucky step-dad I am. One night I came up after the girls, and I found all of Thumper's toys in front of her bed in a straight line, equally spaced and placed by size, no less. "Rebecca, did you do this?" I called. We looked at each other awestruck — had Thumper actually taken inventory?

We moved to a bigger house with our own yard and stairs. Greyhounds love stairs, after you teach them, of course. The first time or two took some coaxing; you'd have thought I was killing her. Thumper can't stay off them now. She runs up and down them with her bunny; not just running but bounding. At first it was rough but, hey, she's a genius. She counts her toys!

I regret to say she doesn't quite know her name, though. She thinks it's "Biscuits," which is another word we can't say unless we really mean it. There's biscuit jars all through the house. She not only knows their locations but the sound each one makes when it's opened. So if you touch one you had best be ready to dish them out. There is nothing like those imploring eyes staring at you after you've inadvertently clanked a jar.

One afternoon on a walk, a mini-van passed us, slammed on the brakes and ended up half on the sidewalk. A woman jumped out and almost ran at us. I prepared myself for either a kidnapping attempt or a barrage of greyhound questions. She turned out to be a fellow adoptee (who owns who?) of a greyhound — in fact, two.

She spoke so highly of her two greyhounds.— how easy they were to take care of and how great they are for each other. By the end of the conversation she'd convinced me to get another one.

I'm thrilled to say I did. Well, we did. The three of us are now 'plus one' two-and-a-half-year-old male we named Emeril. He's been in the house almost a month now. With only a few minor adjustments still needed, he's doing pretty well.

They said two would be easier than one. Not quite yet. Thumper is getting used to competition for affection in the house, and she loves having someone to run up and down the stairs with her all night long. Emeril, however, barks, licks, and sits on the couch. He doesn't know how to eat a biscuit. He chomps with his mouth open spreading biscuit all over the kitchen floor. I wish I had a dime for every piece of biscuit stuck in the bottom of my shoe. Thumper never did any of these things. She's now teaching him how to run stairs, and like I taught her, to play in a crouched position and pounce around, and yes, even eat a biscuit. He in turn is teaching her how to bark, how to lick, how to sit on the couch. So it's back to school for everyone.

Such is life with the greyhounds. How can one deny them? The smile, personality oozing from their eyes, the crazy ways they sniff, hook and keep every greyhound owner for life. (What's the deal with the tip of their nose? It seems like it just kind of swivels around on the end of their face.) They lean when being petted and they sigh when they're happy. They're always at the front door prancing with love and affection, full of zany greyhound antics, when you get home. I find myself talking way too long answering all the questions curious people ask. It seems that half of the pictures I take now have dogs in them. After all, they are part of the family. How did all this happen to me?

I still keep two residences, one in L.A., but I have to tell you that when I'm high above in that airplane there's only three things on my mind: My beautiful Rebecca and my two great kids, Thumper and Emeril. You know, somewhere along the line I made the transition from step-dad to just plain old dad.

Sandy

Pat Burton

I argue that there can be no reason (except the selfish desire
to preserve the privileges of the exploiting group)
for refusing to extend the basic principle of
equality of consideration to members of the other species.
— Pete Singer

ONE DAY IN March the phone rang. Angela (founder of our greyhound rescue team) asked if I could pick up a dog that had been homed in Cheltenham only a week previously and take him to the kennels where our rescues are boarded. I contacted the people who had Sandy, and their specific request was that we pick Sandy up "sooner rather than later." The well-intentioned owners were not confident enough to go out and leave him in the house.

I was met upon arrival by a young tearful couple with a child. The explanation was immediate. "We're sorry to have to part with him, but he's done so much damage." The thin, fawn dog was handed to me with the information that he had had a bath and had a passion for rich tea biscuits!

"Well, Sandy," I said as I packed him into the back of my Land Rover, "I have a few things to do on my way home."

First, I stopped at the supermarket for a quick shop. Nervously conscious of the fawn fellow's presence, I sped round the store with visions of him taking my car apart in my absence! I was pleasantly relieved to find my vehicle intact as I stacked the groceries onto the back seat. Next I had to pick up a friend's daughter from school, which gave me a chance to walk Sandy.

"Oh, you have another dog?" my friend remarked.

"No, no, he's on his way to the kennels," I said.

On the way home I began to wonder if perhaps I could foster Sandy. He seemed to be such a lovely boy, but he was too thin. He would look much more adoptable if he had a little care first.

On arriving home I was greeted by the gang, including Joe, a collie cross greyhound, who had come as a foster dog and stayed.

Sandy and Joe seemed to hit it off. They were well matched in the energy stakes. They spent the next day tearing around, seeing who could outrun who, then rounding up the horses. Not a good idea, boys! As time went by I became very attached to Sandy. Although he was only a young dog, I discovered his past had been eventful, to say the least. He was picked up as a flea-ridden stray in Manchester, then homed in Shropshire, rehomed in London, then again in Shropshire and finally in Cheltenham, where I found him!

I telephoned the young couple in Cheltenham who were so upset to part with him. "Just letting you know that I am keeping Sandy," I informed them. "I know you were fond of him."

"Oh, yes," said the wife, "I'll always remember Sandy. Every time I visit the loo I am reminded of him. I sit there and view his handiwork around the door frame!"

Eight months later Sandy is still with me. How could I resist this charmer with his zest for life? It was time he had a permanent home!

The Sport of Death

Julie Schenk

"Their bodies were scattered," the paper read.
Lean, long-legged greyhounds,
A bullet in each head.

72 greyhounds were found that way
In a garbage-strewn lemon field
On a still winter day.

The dogs were so young — most two or three
What crime did they do
That deserved this cruelty?

The judge was their trainer — the crime was, "Too slow."
The verdict was "Guilty,"
To the death field they'd go.

These trusting dogs were led there that day
By the trainer they'd worked for —
Their trust he'd betray.

Each greyhound was shot as their sentence that day.
For what humans call "Sport,"
What a price these dogs pay!

The Greyhound

Julie Schenk

Greyhounds are
majestic,
powerful,
muscular,
agile,
swift,
intelligent,
good natured,
gentle,
sensitive,
loyal,
trusting,
innocent,
slaughtered like cattle each year.

Life in the Fast Lane

Julie Schenk

Fancy Dan was a racer,
That's all that he knew.
So he ran and he ran,
Till each race was through.

The end of each race
Found him in his crate.
His muzzle removed
Just when he ate.

But losers aren't wanted,
And Dan didn't win.
So he went on a journey
In a truck with some men.

On a shadowed back road,
They unlatched Dan's crate.
A voice echoed, "Get out!"
Fancy Dan didn't wait.

Enchanted with freedom,
Dan ran through the night,
Too excited to see
The truck vanish from sight.

As the morning sun rose
In the sky the next day,

Dan couldn't find water,
Or a cool place to stay.

Half dead from thirst,
Dan did what he knew.
He ran and he ran
'Till the whole day was through.

Feet stinging with pain
From sharp rocks that day,
Dan limped to a farm –
Bullets sent him away.

Done licking his wound,
Dan ran on through the night.
He did what he knew,
though in pain, and with fright.

Afraid and confused,
he stopped running at last.
When out of the woods
came sounds from the past.

The sounds were of vans,
he took to the track,
so he ran to the sounds
that might take him back.

Dan did what he knew,
afraid in the night.

He ran toward the sounds,
but was blinded by light.

When the night turned to day,
And the bright day was new,
Fancy Dan ran no longer.
His race was now through.

Fancy Dan was a greyhound
Who ran his life through
Thrown away by his trainer
When he was just two.

Indie

Pat Burton

Non-violence leads to the highest ethics, which is
the goal of all evolution. Until we stop harming all
other living beings, we are still savages.

— *Thomas Edison*

INDIE'S IS A sad story indeed. She arrived with her four surviving puppies, apparently having laid on four others with fatal
consequences. Perhaps it was nature's way of culling because
Indie was in no fit state to nurse puppies.

She was dirty and neglected, and she had mange... All of
this could be treated, but what about a broken jaw? How
could this happen? Had she been cold, hungry and barking in
desperation, only to be punished with a brutal kicking?

A stable was prepared for Indie's arrival, with a heat lamp
ready. She was made as comfortable as possible and a night-
long vigil began. Morning brought more anxiety; two of the
pups were cold and barely alive. A warming up process began
in earnest with hot water bottles and bottle feedings but to no

avail. Neither survived. The remaining two puppies seemed all right and somehow I felt confident that they would make it. The two survivors, one black and the other white, were christened Ebony and Ivory. Indie was a good mother despite all of her own problems.

Indie had a prospective home lined up with an ex-veterinary nurse who wanted that name for her. Her new mum wanted to nurse Indie and give her the love and attention she had lacked in her life. As with all our rescued dogs, she was to be spayed. I booked her into the vet for the operation and asked if her jaw could be x-rayed while under the anesthetic. Sores had also appeared around her mouth. The vet diagnosed disease of the jaw bone and antibiotics were prescribed. During the period after the operation, before the stitches were due to be removed, Indie's condition deteriorated and she had difficulty eating. I became concerned, and upon her return to the vet she was diagnosed with cancer.

Tearfully I drove home that night. The next day Indie made her final journey to the vet. She fell peacefully asleep on the very day we had scheduled to give her a home. What a brutal world she had experienced!

Historical Perspective

Susan Netboy

The greyhound: swift as the wind, elegant as a gazelle. Throughout its renowned six thousand year history, the greyhound has been celebrated for its loyalty, speed and beauty, distinctions which earned the breed the status of noble coursing hound and the patronage of kings. As exclusive property of the aristocracy, the greyhound was treasured and protected for centuries — until the breed's unique athletic abilities collided headlong with 20th century greed. The once noble greyhound began running for its life.

With the advent of pari-mutuel betting on greyhound racing in the 1920s, the greyhound acquired a new master. The multi-million-dollar racing industry was a master with an insatiable appetite for more money and more and more dogs. The breeding frenzy that followed sealed the degradation of the breed. The greyhound now garnered a new distinction as an exploited disposable commodity that was rewarded for its service to the industry with a cruel and ignoble death at an early age.

Government officials, eager for quick fix budget remedies,

welcomed state revenues skimmed off the backs of these canine athletes. Following the industry's lead, they too ignored
the fate of the entities from which they profited. Once the
industry was entrenched, each year thousands upon thousands
of doe-eyed greyhounds joined the muzzled inmates of the
seamy, insular world of greyhound racing.

For most, death would be the only relief from the often
tick and flea infested cages which were their "homes." Those
cages were quickly filled with new victims of the "race against
death." The unpromising, the sick, the injured would be the
first to go, but the same fate would ultimately befall the veter-
ans as soon as their money making potential began to fade.
During the first 50 years of its existence, the dog racing industry, unimpeded by outside scrutiny or ethical misgivings, was
content to rake in huge profits from an enterprise which has
been responsible for the routine killing of hundreds of thousands of innocent greyhounds. This, in turn, spawned a cottage
industry of executioners who operated "kill truck runs" to
dispose of unprofitable greyhounds. Though a few dogs were
spared for breeding, the majority were shipped off by truck-
load to research facilities and dog pounds, or disappeared in
the middle of the night to be disposed of by the cheapest
means available.

The grim fate which awaited nearly every racing greyhound for decades began to change for a few in the mid 1980s,
when a handful of enlightened individuals tangentially associ-
ated with the racing industry started to adopt former racing
greyhounds into homes. Soon rescuers from all walks of life
emerged to champion the greyhound as a pet. As word of the
sweet, gentle nature of the greyhound spread, the adoption
effort expanded throughout the country and sparked a national outcry about the plight of the racing greyhound. Media
coverage of greyhound abuse cases was catapulted from ob-

scurity to the front pages of newspapers and TV screens across the country. By the 1990s, the greyhound racing industry found itself in the crosshairs of intense media scrutiny and the object of relentless public criticism.

Facing a public relations disaster that posed a patent threat to profits, the industry hired a public relations firm. They then stepped forward, check in hand, to proclaim that greyhound welfare and adoption were the industry's primary concern. This stereotypical image makeover was a classic case of too little too late. The American public had already turned its back on dog racing.

As industry profits and attendance continue to plummet, forcing the closure of one track after another, the greyhound racing industry is now "running for its life." This final chapter will be welcomed by many as a suitable ending to a very unsuitable business.

Would a Greyhound
Be the Right Dog for Me?

There is no more important decision than the decision to adopt
and assume responsibility for another life. That decision carries an
obligation to nurture that life... to give it love... to care for it.
— Roger Caras

FOR ALL OF you who are wondering about whether a greyhound is the dog for you, the following is a collection of the
most commonly asked questions and their answers:

Q. What qualities make a racing greyhound a good pet?
A. They are friendly, affectionate, gentle, quiet, sweet, loyal,
   clean, loving, sensitive, trusting and good natured.

Q. How long will it take for an adult greyhound to bond
   with the new owner and adjust to life as a pet?
A. Greyhounds are very friendly and thrive on human companionship. Consequently, bonding is usually established
   within a matter of days, and getting used to a new environment and routine may take a few weeks. The older
   dogs tend to be better mannered from the start, while the
   younger dogs are generally more curious and active.

Q. Is a racing greyhound difficult to housetrain?

A. At the track, racing greyhounds are accustomed to being let out of their crates several times a day to relieve themselves. Because of this, a similar routine in a new home makes housetraining relatively easy. When the adopter employs patience and common sense, the greyhound's natural cleanliness will assist in the process. The use of an airline crate can be of great assistance in helping the dog adjust to a new routine and environment.

Q. What provisions need to be furnished by the adopter?

A. A greyhound needs a safe, warm environment, good quality food, basic annual veterinary care, a soft bed, and lots of love.

Q. What ages are available and what is the life expectancy of a racing greyhound?

A. Most are between two and five years of age. The average life expectancy of a former racing greyhound is 12-15 years.

Q. What is the size of a racing greyhound?

A. Racing greyhounds stand between 24 and 28 inches at the shoulder, and they weigh between 50 and 80 pounds. Females are usually smaller than males.

Q. What are the colors of a greyhound?

A. Black, fawn, red, blue, several shades of brindle, and white, with a combination of these colors.

Q. Are greyhounds good with children?

A. They are better than most breeds, but not as tolerant as some. If a child becomes overbearing they will usually walk away rather than snap or growl. However, every dog has its limits. Because greyhounds are gentle by nature, most are fine with children 8 and older who have been taught respect for animals. Most adoption groups are hesitant to place a dog in a family with toddlers unless there is specific assurance that strict supervision will be provided over both child and dog.

Q. Are greyhounds good with other dogs?

A. They are friendly by nature and socialize well as a result of their exposure to other greyhounds at the kennels. Adopters should advise their adoption counselor about the other breeds of dogs living in the household. Also, common sense must be exercised during the introductory period and with regard to food. Feeding separately recommended.

Q. Are racing greyhounds compatible with cats?

A. About half of track greyhounds that come into adoption programs can be placed with cats. Adoption groups test the cat socializing skill of each dog before placing it.

Q. Why do greyhounds have to be kept on a leash?

A. All dogs should be on leash near traffic or other hazards. The greyhound follows its instincts and runs without heed and therefore can be off leash only when in a large fenced area.

Q. Can greyhounds be obedience trained?

A. Many former racing greyhounds have earned obedience titles. However, greyhounds do not possess the same predilection for taking commands as the working breeds. All training must be done with a light encouraging hand. Positive reinforcement and/or food are the best incentives for both formal and informal training. Leash rules must be heeded, even with a highly obedience trained greyhound, as voice control is not sufficient in a dangerous situation.

Q. Why must greyhounds be spayed or neutered?

A. With thousands of greyhounds dying each year in spite of nationwide adoption efforts, it would be unthinkable and irresponsible to allow more breeding to occur.

Q. Are greyhounds hyperactive?

A. No. The most common misconception about racing greyhounds is that a dog capable of great athletic feats is a dog in perpetual motion. In reality, they are rather lazy and greatly enjoy lounging with the family.

Q. Do racing greyhounds require a lot of exercise?

A. They enjoy, but are not dependent on, moderate exercise. They make good jogging companions after they are properly conditioned for long distances. In most households, the shared experience of a brisk walk is enough to keep both the adopter and the adoptee in good physical health.

Q. Do females make better pets than males?

A. No, males and females make equally good pets. The females are generally more independent, and the males are somewhat more affectionate.

Q. Will adopting a greyhound change my life?

A. Yes. You will have the satisfaction of having saved a life and will gain the companionship of a devoted, affectionate and loyal friend.

About Our Contributors

Barber, Kevin

Kevin is a musician. He and his band perform through-out the greater Los Angeles area. He has written several articles and short stories for Greyhound Today magazine and other publications. Currently working and living part time in Los Angeles, he calls Alameda, California, in the Bay Area, his home. This is the place where his darling Rebecca and their two "kids" live. Although he is only there one week per month, home is after all where the heart is.

Burton, Pat

Pat has been fostering greyhounds as a trustee of Grey-hound West of England for about two years. By now she has fostered many dogs, and of course a few have become perma-nently hers. She wishes she could keep them all.

Coleman, Louise

On Mothers Day in 1983, Louise, a rehabilitation counse-lor for the U.S. Department of Labor, visited Wonderland Race Track in Revere, Massachusetts at the urging of an acquaintance who knew that a discarded racer was due to be killed shortly. Though she had no previous experience with greyhounds, Louise adopted "Boston Boy" who received the new name "Shadow," and another chance at life. Shortly after this, with the help of several volunteers, Louise started the work of Greyhound Friends, a small non-profit organization dedicated to saving racing greyhounds. The organization was incorporated in Boston, Massachusetts two years later, and since that time almost 7000 retired racers have found good and caring homes.

In the past few years Greyhound Friends, Inc. has been able to increase its geographical base and affiliate with five other adoption centers in the country. Also, Greyhound Friends of Ireland has been started in Glenlohane, the home of Desmond and Melanie Sharp Bolster in Cork, with the help of Greyhound Friends and Irish residents interested in greyhound welfare.

Louise has received the Reverence for Life Award of the New England Antivivisection Society, and the Courage of Conscience Award by the Peace Abbey.

Combest, Hope

Hope is the founder and chairwoman of the board for the Greyhound Rescue Society of Texas, Inc. She became involved with greyhounds in 1991 and to this day oversees the operation of the organization. Her love and concern for the retired racing greyhounds has given her the incentive and determination to continue in her original mission to see to it that all unwanted greyhounds get a second chance at life by finding them loving and secure homes.

Hope works in Waco, Texas as an administrative assistant for a non-profit organization which provides social service to at-risk students and their families.

Devens, Scotti

In 1991 Scotti met and adopted her first greyhound and began learning of their plight. She decided instantly to commit to the saving of these gentle, noble dogs. She founded "Save the Greyhound Dogs! Inc.," in her home state of Vermont. Scotti was instrumental in the banning of racing in her state with the introduction of the "Gator Bill" signed into law in 1995. (So named because of her dog Gator) In December 1995, Scotti received the Humane Society of the United States legislative achievement award for getting the Gator Bill into law.

Scotti states that her commitment is so strong that she will not stop until greyhound racing is banned nationally. She quotes one of her heroes, Sir Winston Churchill, "You ask, what is our goal? It is victory, no matter how long and hard the road may be."

Dugan, Alex

Alex lives in Northern California with his wife and two greyhounds, Max and Melissa. He teaches computer science at a community college and enjoys writing and photography in his spare time. Alex says he likes a quote by Harry Truman which is "I never give them hell, I just tell the truth and they think it's hell!" Maybe apropos of this story collection.

Emery, Lauren

Lauren did the photos of Bernie and Boomer. Both dogs were adopted through Greyhound Placement Service of Maine and for the last four years Lauren has done many adoption demonstrations. She feels that the hard work, which is fun for the dogs, has introduced many people to the wonderful world of greyhounds enabling them to get the retirement they deserve.

Finch, B. Anne

Anne became aware of the plight of the greyhound in 1986 when she adopted an ex-racer, Emma, from a refuge where a third of the inmates were greyhounds and lurchers. Researching Emma's earmarks and origins, Anne stumbled onto the sad world of greyhound racing and the tragedy of so many unwanted ex-racers. She joined others in campaigning for a better life for these beautiful creatures and she helped home hundreds of them. She became more and more alarmed by the tales she heard of the dogs exported from Ireland to Spain and in 1991 planned a secret visit to observe the condition and bring back four dogs to England through quarantine. Her report stopped the trade for five months pending an inspection by the World Greyhound Federation. Over the next five years she made thirteen more visits, working alongside the people there in an effort to teach proper care, producing an instructional video in Spanish and bringing out fifty dogs to homes in northern Europe. She also traveled to Morocco where Irish dogs are exported and helped liaise with an animal welfare group in South Africa to help prevent the legislation of greyhound racing there.

Mrs. Finch started out life as a music teacher and pianist, then turned to nursing which she has been doing full-time for thirty years. She is married to a university professor.

Harkin, Karen

Karen has been a sighthound fan for many years. While living in Iowa, she was a foster mom for several greyhounds. Her current greyhound, Posey Troubles, was a replacement for a whippet, a long-time pal, who died in 1992. Karen has been involved with hunter and jumper horses and ponies for over 30 years. Currently, while not performing her duties for a housing developer, she supports her 10-year-old daughter, Tina with her riding efforts.

Lander, Cheryl

Cheryl received a Masters in Spirituality degree from Santa Clara University in 1993. Her thesis was on developing an Ecospirituality. She approaches spirituality in an inclusive manner: humans are in partnership with the rest of creation. She believes that developing a deeper appreciation for the interconnectedness of all life is a joyful, healing experience.

She lives in San Jose, California with her husband and two dogs; Liz, an airedale and Mozart, a husky. Her greyhound, Lance, has gone to heaven. She hopes to have another greyhound soon.

Lint, Bee

Bee is a Pawnee Indian who is a member of Greyhound Friends for Life. She is a retired nurse and has been writing poetry and caring for animals most of her life. She has adopted two greyhounds and prefers to work with those who need special handling and care. "Some are more traumatized and need much more attention than others — as an Indian, I can relate to that," she says. She lives with her dogs by the waters of Clear Lake, California. Earlier in her life she fostered dogs for the Animal Protection League.

Linzey, Professor Andrew

We used one of his quotes in the book. He holds the first fellowship in theology and animal welfare, the International Fund for Animal Welfare senior research fellowship at Mansfield College, Oxford. Widely regarded as the leading theologian on animal issues, his first book, "Animal Rights" also was a part of the beginning of the animal rights movement.

Another of his quotes we like is as follows: "The idea that animals are here for our use has a long history. The new idea that there are moral limits to what we should do to animals

107

has been a long time coming and in its practical implications will appear radical and uncompromising. Nowhere is this clearer than in our use of animals in scientific research."

Marks, Jane

Jane lives in San Carlos, California with her husband and son, and of course their greyhound Bonnie.

Marsh, Greta

Greta was a probation officer in Nassau County, New York for over twenty years. She worked with troubled and abused youngsters and battered women. During this time she became aware of the abuse and slaughter of horses. There are eight slaughter houses in the U.S. Upon retiring in late 1991 in Massachusetts, she built a barn and started rescuing horses on a small scale. To date rescues include a show horse, pacer, polo pony, companion horse and two race horses, the latter ages three and four. The three-year-old was taken off the killers' truck.

In December 1991 she adopted Shayna from Greyhound Friends of Maine, a four-year-old former racer who had been abandoned while wearing her racing muzzle, in a Maine cemetery. She started protesting at New England dog tracks, primarily Green Mountain in Vermont, then met with state representative Shaun Kelly, who agreed to file a bill to abolish dog racing in Maine. HB899 was filed in December 1994 and died in July 1996, along with other racing bills. It made quite an impact however. Its file in the office of the Joint Committee on government regulations is about 10 inches thick and contains mail in favor of abolition.

Greta strongly believes that human and non-human animal abuse are extremely closely connected. "Where you find one, you usually find the other."

Mastrocola, Kari

Kari has always been involved with dogs including greyhounds. She began to show dogs at age seven and became one of the top junior handlers in the nation. She has worked at top greyhound and sighthound kennels in England and Australia. Later she became interested in the plight of the racing greyhound and became involved in rescue work with Greyhound Friends for Life in California. The idea of doing this book was hers.

Meier, Bruce

Bruce lives with his wife and their two greyhounds in the San Francisco bay area. They keep in touch with many Greyhound Friends for Life at annual picnics and through other associations and activities.

Netboy, Susan

Susan's involvement in the greyhound issue evolved out of her rescue efforts for sighthound breeds. Her discovery in September 1989 that greyhounds slated for military ballistic experiments were sold without the knowledge or consent of the legal owners, forced the U.S. Army to release 19 racing greyhounds for placement into pet homes.

Suspecting that these greyhounds represented the tip of the iceberg, Susan acquired additional documents through the Freedom of Information Act and spend the next two years tracing the ownership of some 600 greyhounds sold to various research laboratories throughout the west. Her investigative work and persistence led to lawsuits which secured the liberation of dozens of greyhounds and focused national attention on the widespread sale of "retired" greyhounds to laboratories.

The investigative process also unveiled to Susan the dark underside of the greyhound racing industry and detailed insider accounts of the brutal realities facing greyhounds caught in the racing system. Haunted by this knowledge and determined to address the core issues behind the plight of the racing greyhound, Susan founded the Greyhound Protection League, a national greyhound advocacy group; the National Greyhound Adoption Network, a national referral service, and Greyhound Friends for Life, a California-based rescue organization.

Susan has been in the forefront of the greyhound adoption effort and a pioneer in the movement to end the suffering of the racing greyhounds nationwide.

Owens, Kim

Kim makes her home in South Carolina with her husband and three greyhounds. Her husband runs their antique store while Kim teaches computers at a local vocational school. She is also active in freelance writing in the antique trade and is the author of the column, "Computers and the Antiques," seen regularly in the publication "AntiqueWeek." They have recently begun fostering greyhounds and plan to continue acclimating these great dogs to their retirement. Angel, Stubby, and Sunshine still thrive in their lazy southern climate and live quite peacefully with a tiny Himalayan kitty named Cleopatra.

With any time left Kim repairs antique beaded necklaces, hunts greyhound antiques, or takes the dogs on joyous romps in a nearby fenced field. She welcomes e-mail and enjoys nothing more than talking about her "babies." Her addresses are:

MomtoAngel@aol.com *or* FlounderDogs@ais-gwd.com

Presto, Caudia

Claudia happily gave up her New York corporate life to travel west with her five-year-old greyhound, Slim, whom she adopted in 1985. She was seeking land and freedom where she could rescue greyhounds from racing and have the freedom to care for them and find them homes. She settled in Kanab, Utah where she established her "Greyhound Gang" a nonprofit organization dedicated to rescuing, rehabilitating and adopting out greyhounds.

Claudia has written a "Top Ten List" for greyhounds as follows:

10. *They don't slobber.*
9. *They hardly shed.*
8. *They like to be with kids.*
7. *They're the fastest dogs on the block but don't brag about it.*
6. *They're bigger couch potatoes than you are.*
5. *They could qualify for Mensa (most of them).*
4. *They're unfailingly sweet and polite.*
3. *They don't smell like dogs.*
2. *They look you in the eye when you talk to them.*
1. *They're forever thankful to you for saving their lives.*

Rippe, Alexis

Alexis lives in the great "banana belt" of southeast Alaska. She is surrounded by fjords, glaciers, huge evergreens, bears, and bald eagles. There are no roads in or out except by sky or sea. They experience unique problems like waiting for the barge to bring milk and bread and if the planes can't fly, the mail gets very backed up in bad weather.

Alexis has been involved with dogs for 16 years. She became interested in obedience five years ago and in 1995, Yukon, her French bulldog, was #1 for the breed in Canada in obedience. He was also #2 Delaney (an obedience ranking system based on the number of dogs you have defeated) for the breed in the U.S. She pays her bills by working for the City and Borough as a Firefighter.

Roth, Bill

Bill is a product manager for the scientific instrument division of Hitachi Corporation of Japan. For about 15 years he had an American Saddlebred horse which he enjoyed jumping, showing and trail riding. After the horse passed away, his interests turned to dogs. He was moved by the story of Greyhound Friends for Life, and the rest is history.

Ruge, Christin

Our beloved greyhound Mindy is no longer the newest member of our family. Matthew was born in February 1997 and our two dogs are very protective of the new baby. Max, our ten-year-old Springer Spaniel, acts as if he is the mother. Mindy is a little more shy around the baby, but still mimics Max's antics by "kissing" the baby. The dogs continue to be a very important part of our life. The walks we share are among our most treasured moments, and they have been incorporated into most of our recreation time including rollerblading, yard work, watching movies (at home of course) and entertaining friends. Our once-shy greyhound now excitedly greets our friends and cuddles next to them if they let her. Going for a car ride has become as fun for Mindy as our walks, so now I have a wonderful companion when I run my errands.

Schenk, Julie

Julie is a 15-year-old high school student from Maryland who chose to research greyhound racing for her term paper. As she learned the shameful truth of the racing industry, she was moved to write the three poems included in this book. Julie is hoping that her poetry will help to show the public the truth of the cruelty inherent in racing.

Stahl, Gary

Gary resides in Fresno, California with his wife and daughter. His greyhound "Freedom" has been with him for two years. He saved her with the help of Greyhound Friends for Life. She has not only been a blessing in their lives, but has filled their hearts with love.

Star, Nora

Nora has been active in animal welfare issues all of her life — both hands-on and through the written word. Two years ago she wrote "My Greyhound Friend" after working with these dogs for a few years fostering them in her home. It is a short story for children of any age. She has written numerous short stories and newspaper articles, usually somehow related to the animal realm. Since learning of the plight of the greyhound, her writing has been almost exclusively about them. She shares her home with her husband, one beagle, and two greyhounds. They often have greyhound friend visitors, both the two legged and four legged types.

Nora loves to communicate via e-mail with anyone about animal issues or writing. Her address is: Startimm@pacific.net

She supports local animal welfare groups and also is a docent at the local state park in addition to her first love which is greyhound rescue.

Nora collected and edited the stories for this book.

Wolner, Bobbi

Bobbi is a children's librarian who began her greyhound rescue with Susie, and now has a companion greyhound, Salty Dog. There are also seven cats in the household, most of whom were someone else's throwaways and became Bobbi's treasures. Animals and nature are very important parts of her life and she feels fortunate to be able to devote time to both.

If you wish to respond to any of our contributors, please send letters to me:

Nora Star
9728 Tenaya Way
Kelseyville, CA 95451

I will forward them.

Resources

For more information about adopting greyhounds or help-ing their cause, check these sources:

NGAN (National Greyhound Adoption Network).
  Dial 1-800-G-HOUNDS.
  This organization can direct you to the rescue people in your particular locality, and tell you of their of capabilities.

Greyhound Network News is an independently published quar-terly newsletter dedicated to reporting news and related issues pertaining to racing greyhounds. *GNN* is a concise, eight-page source of information compiled from various sources both national and international. Each issue follows a consis-tent format and in general contains: state-by-state news, legis-lative updates, track openings and closings, industry econom-ics, international news, letters to the editor, photo essays, and feature articles as space allows.

  GNN began publication in 1992 in response to the massa-cre of 143 racing greyhounds whose decomposing bodies were discovered in an abandoned orchard in Chandler Heights, less than thirty miles from downtown Phoenix, Arizona. In the years since then the racing industry has experienced an overall eco-nomic decline and is unlikely to recover due to the enormous competition from the rapidly expanding casino gaming mar-ket and the greater spread of information surfacing in the national media regarding the cruelties involved in this "sport".

There is now a growing national grassroots movement working toward the elimination of greyhound racing and results so far have been impressive. Five states — Maine, Virginia, Vermont, Idaho and Washington — have enacted legislation banning greyhound racing. Two of those states, Vermont and Idaho, were formerly racing states. More states are expected to follow as bills to ban this sport make their way through other state legislatures.

While GNN is primarily a news information source, it also stands as a written testament to the grim business that currently accounts for the deaths, often inhumane, of 25,000 to 30,000 racing greyhounds per year in the United States.

Greyhound Network News is free to anyone interested in or already involved in greyhound advocacy. However, the newsletter is dependent on reader contributions to cover printing and postage costs. GNN is a non-profit 501 (c) (3) Arizona corporation and contributions are tax-deductible.

To receive a brochure about the newsletter or a sample copy, write to: Greyhound Network News, P.O. Box 44272, Phoenix, AZ 85064

For additional copies of

Greyhound Tales:
True Stories of Rescue, Compassion and Love

Send $15.95 plus $1.00 for shipping to:

Nora Star, 9728 Tenaya Way, Kelseyville, CA 95451

To order a copy of a small children's book for any age written by Nora Star, called *My Greyhound Friend,* send $5.95 (no shipping charge) to the same address.

A large portion of the proceeds from both books will be donated to help the greyhound cause.